TRAMPING HOLIDAYS
IN SCOTLAND

TRAMPING HOLIDAYS
IN SCOTLAND

*Twelve walking tours described
in detail by*

TOM S. HALL

Maps by Leo Vernon

LONDON: COUNTRY LIFE LTD
2–10 TAVISTOCK STREET, COVENT GARDEN, W.C.2

First Published 1933
Revised and enlarged edition 1948

MADE AND PRINTED IN GREAT BRITAIN BY
MORRISON AND GIBB LTD., LONDON AND EDINBURGH

CONTENTS

LIST OF ILLUSTRATIONS

LIST OF MAPS

Drawn by Leo Vernon

LIST OF MAPS

PREFACE

THE second and revised edition bears little resemblance to the first edition. The original script contained five tours, but the number has now been increased to twelve. The Arran tour has been withdrawn because it is given in greater detail elsewhere. The other four tours which appeared in the first issue have been " streamlined " so far as words are concerned, but the essential details remain. The routes of these tours have been checked, but one drawback at the present time is that full facilities have not yet been restored for travel. Be careful therefore to check up transport facilities in advance.

The Cairngorm and Grampian tours revive in me happy memories of the war years spent on work in the forests of those districts. Many wild days we spent there in winter time, when the snow lay very deep for weeks on end.

Frankly, the place names have become a nightmare. The spelling seems to change in all sorts of unexpected ways, and in spite of repeated checking and re-checking it is possible you may find a word that, to you, has been spelt incorrectly. I am not an authority on the spelling of place names, but it should be borne in mind that the spelling given in every case is according to the Ordnance Survey map. The spelling of a name is not necessarily the same on different maps, and I cannot say which is the correct spelling. So, if you think I have spelt a name incorrectly you may be right, but if you find that my spelling is the same as that on the Ordnance map, then that is the way in which I intended to spell the word. I am all for simplified spelling. I would like to see such a word as " Ben " always spelt in one way, but sometimes it is spelt on the map as BEN and another time as BEINN.

The maps are included merely to give a general picture of the area to be visited, and, of course, are not intended to act as guide maps. One or two exceptions have been made in place-name spellings in the maps. One instance is that the old spelling Criffel has been given on the map on page 37 whereas the Ordnance Survey spelling Criffell is given in the text.

I wish to express my thanks to the staff at the Dundee Reference Library; for about three months they were untiring in helping me in every possible way.

The biggest section of all is the Argyll National Forest Park chapter. The data presented could not have been prepared except with the help of the Forestry Commission, and my thanks are due to all those who helped me, from the officials at the Edinburgh office to those working in the forest.

Also I want to express my grateful appreciation to a group of schoolmasters in Galloway for the help they gave so readily in checking the tour of this area.

Finally I must include thanks to my son and daughter, who did a lot of routine work for me in the preparation of the book and who accompanied me on some of the excursions, especially the forest walks.

TOM S. HALL.

4 HEUGH STREET,
FALKIRK.

Any reference in this book to a road, track or footpath is not evidence of the existence of a Right-of-Way.

I

THE SCOTT COUNTRY

INTRODUCTION

THIS tour embraces the south-east corner of Scotland generally referred to as The Scott Country. It commences at Berwick-upon-Tweed and follows the coastline as far as Fast Castle, from which point the route turns west to come to the Scott Country at St. Boswells, Melrose, etc. After winding your way through the valleys and over the hills throughout this country you will end by travelling by bus to Edinburgh, where the tour ends. There are only eleven days of walking because it is felt that at the end of the fortnight the visitor should have an opportunity of exploring Edinburgh.

First day.

Travel to Berwick-upon-Tweed.

Second day.

BURNMOUTH AND EYEMOUTH

Route in brief : Berwick-upon-Tweed—Steps of Grace—Catch-a-Penny Burn—Burnmouth—Eyemouth.

Walking distance : 10 miles.

Map : Ordnance Survey 1″ scale, No. 75.

The start of this walk is from the Coastguard Station. Here a footpath leads across the golf links and round by Sharper's Head to Brotherston's Hole, beyond which the path follows the line of the cliffs to Needles Eye. The path now turns inland, crossing under the railway to join the main road. Here you have more than a mile of walking before you come to the notice at the roadside stating that on the one hand is England and on the other is Scotland, after which the main

road follows high up above the sea for several miles.   One
feature of this rock-bound coast is the quaint names given to
the rocks, caves and headlands, and the quaintest of all is
that given to a stream that flows into the sea at Burnmouth,
Catch-a-Penny.   When in Burnmouth you may be able to
ascertain the reason for this name.   A little south from this
fishing village is a rock called the Maiden's Stone, and in the
village itself there is another called Annie's Rock.   To the
north of Burnmouth, at Breeches Rock, a portion of the beach
is known as the King's Garden.   At the point where the main
road, along which you are walking, is above Burnmouth you
come to a road fork.   Turn to the right, and immediately you
see the turning downhill to Burnmouth.

It is necessary to return the same way, but you will discover
that it is worth while.   The fishing village of Burnmouth is
tucked away at the foot of the cliffs and is not visible from the
main road except at a point where you look down the Catch-a-
Penny Burn.   After visiting Burnmouth you return to the
main road, where about two and a half miles of walking brings
you to Eyemouth.   It would be preferable to follow the
cliff-edge, but this is not permissible.   If the main road becomes
monotonous you will be more than compensated when arriving
in Eyemouth, for it is a particularly quaint fishing village and
fits in well with the rocky nature of the coast.   First of all
you should know it is at Eyemouth that kippers are made.
Here you will see the kippering house where the fish, fresh
from the catch, are gutted and smoked.

The Eye Water, the mouth of which forms the harbour of
Eyemouth, comes down from the Lammermuir Hills and
makes a way through the woods of Dean from Ayton before
finally reaching the sea at Eyemouth.   The entrance to the
harbour calls for good seamanship on the part of the fisherman,
and when the sea is rough it is a thrilling sight to see the boats
making for the harbour.   The entrance to the harbour seems
to be bristling with rocks, and great skill is necessary to
negotiate them.   It has been said that " Eyemouth has a dark,
cunning look, is full of alleys, blind and otherwise."   True,
you will not find it so full of colour as other places, but it is
quaint and picturesque and full of interest.   The Fort is a
name given to the promontory overlooking the harbour and

BURNMOUTH

Robert M. Adam

THE EILDON HILLS

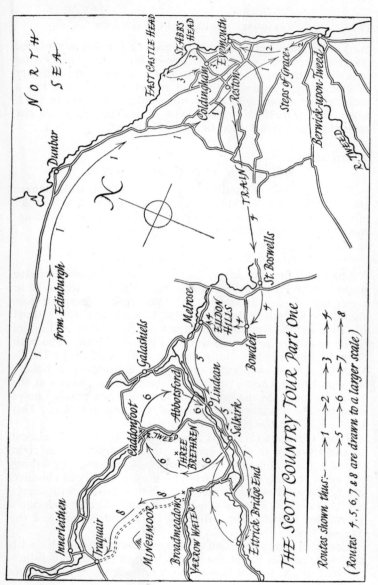

THE SCOTT COUNTRY TOUR Part One

Routes shown thus:— →1 →2 →3 →4
                      →5 →6 →7 →8

(Routes 4, 5, 6, 7 & 8 are drawn to a larger scale)

NORTH SEA

Dunbar

from Edinburgh

EAST CASTLE HEAD

ST ABB'S HEAD

Coldingham

Reston

Eyemouth

Steps of Grace

Berwick-upon-Tweed

R. TWEED

TRAIN

St. Boswells

Galashiels

Melrose

EILDON HILLS

Bowden

Abbotsford

Lindean

Selkirk

Innerleithen

Traquair

Caddonfoot

R. TWEED

THREE BRETHREN

MINCHMOOR

Broadmeadows

YARROW WATER

Ettrick Bridge End

marks the site where Cromwell erected a fortification placed under the control of the Governor of Berwick. The herring industry of Eyemouth appears to have succeeded the industry of smuggling. According to old reports every house has a secret cellar where contraband was hidden, but even in 1792, when the *Statistical Account* was drawn up, most of the smugglers had either died or left the district.

Third day.

ST. ABB'S AND FAST CASTLE

Route in brief: Coastline from Eyemouth to Coldingham Bay and St. Abb's—Mire Loch—Coldingham Loch—Telegraph Hill—Fast Castle—Dow Law—Lumsdaine—Coldingham—bus to Eyemouth.

Walking distance: 17 miles.

Map: Ordnance Survey 1″ scale, No. 75.

The route for this day is more than the average of twelve miles but, if Fast Castle is to be included, it is necessary to cover the mileage as stated. At Eyemouth a footpath goes round to Killiedraft Bay and then turns inland for a short distance before coming back again to the beach at Linkim Stone, standing at the mouth of Hallydown Dean. The path from Linkim wanders along the line of the cliff to the De'il's Dander, which is a gully crossed by a small and rickety wooden bridge known to some of the children visitors as the Fairy Bridge. On the far side of this gully is a grassy knowe marking the southern extremity of Coldingham Bay. This knowe is called the Hamely Knoll.

From Coldingham Sands a path winds up the cliffs almost to the entrance of The Haven, and then bears to the right round by the cliff edge to Neptune's Rock and the fishing village of St. Abb's. The harbour seems to have been chiselled out of the solid rock and the entrance to it bristles with sharp, tooth-like rocks, most of which are named. There are Jonah's Rock, the Thistley Brigs, Big and Little Green Carr and the Treadle Rock.

Continue along the road proper connecting St. Abb's with the outer world, but a few yards beyond the church follow the path to the right which brings you back again to the cliff-edge at Halterums Loup at the far side of the Bell Hill. The path follows the Raven's Brae to the west side of Mire Loch, and so to the woodlands of St. Abb's, where at one time a nunnery stood. No traces of the building are now visible. From the headland you will work round the bay called Pettico Wick and cross the moorland to Coldingham Loch, where you come to the main road ending at Westerside. Here you must cross the moorland again and bear north-west to Lumsdaine Farm for the track to Telegraph Hill, whence you look down to Fast Castle Head and the ruins of Fast Castle itself, which is approachable by one path only, bordered on either side by the cliffs. Sir Walter Scott in his *Provincial Antiquities* tells the story of the castle, stating that it was the stronghold of Logan Wrestlerigg. There is much of interest to tell regarding this castle and those who wish to read more are referred to Sir Walter Scott's works. From Telegraph Hill you have a wide view of the rock-bound coast; to the north is the lighthouse beyond Cockburnspath, and North Berwick and the Bass Rock. For the return journey it is necessary to retrace your steps to Lumsdaine Farm. Instead, however, of cutting across the moorland again to Coldingham Loch you follow the road connecting Lumsdaine with Coldingham, whence you travel by bus to Eyemouth.

Fourth day.

TO THE SCOTT COUNTRY

Route in brief : Eyemouth—Reston Station—Train to St. Boswells—walk to Bowden and over the Eildon Hills to Melrose.

Walking distance : 12 miles.

Maps : Ordnance Survey 1" scale, Nos. 75, 80 and 81.

You require to make an early start for this excursion if you intend to travel by the morning train from Reston Station. There are few trains, and to miss the early one somewhat upsets the plans for the day. From Eyemouth you have six miles of walking before you come to Reston and the route you follow is along the secondary road by way of Highlaws Farm and the cross-roads at Ale Mill. Here you turn to the left and, almost at once, turn to the right to the next cross-roads beyond Whitfield Farm. Your route now will be to turn to the left to Cairncross and on to the main road near Heugh Head. A little more than half a mile of walking brings you to Reston Station.

You arrive at St. Boswells Station well before lunch, travelling down the border through Chirnside, Duns, Greenlaw, Coldstream and Kelso. (Confirm the train times.)

The station of St. Boswells is not situated at St. Boswells at all but at the village of Newtown. From the station at Newtown follow the road to Bowden, which bears away to the left at the County Rooms. All the way you have the Bowden Burn on your right and the Eildon Hills ahead and a little to the left. At the schoolhouse at Bowden turn up to the right and follow the by-way, which soon becomes a footpath, past the smithy to the Curling Pond. Here the footpath forks. You follow the right-hand path, which crosses the rising ground to the reservoir, where you are on the edge of the moorland. A short distance farther on, another footpath crosses at right angles—follow the right-hand path up to the Little Hill, beyond which you cut through Eildon Midhill and Eildon Westerhill, the higher of which is 1,385 feet. Soon after this the path begins to descend; you follow the dividing path to the left to come to the Siller Stone, beyond which is the Broad Wood. You are near the summit now and further direction is unnecessary. The path is well marked and ere long you are on the tops of the Eildon Hills. Crowning the highest point there is a view indicator to help you to identify the many hills, and it is left to you to add the adjectives and superlatives necessary to describe the wide, spreading aspect.

You have a choice of ways down to Melrose. If you turn to the left when descending, you strike a well-defined footpath that brings you to the Gallows Brae and a road leading under a bridge to the cross at the head of the High Street. If you descend to the right from the summit, you come to Horse shoe Plantation and a path that joins the hill road at the head of Eildon Tree Plantation. At the foot of these woodlands is the Eildon Tree Stone, marking the site of the trysting-tree by the roadside. The hill road brings you to the main road, where, by turning to the right, you have one and a half miles of walking before reaching Melrose High Street.

Apart from the superb position of Melrose and the wooded loveliness of the surrounding district, the chief attraction is the Abbey, founded in 1136 for the Cistercian monks.

In the quiet of the evening it is good to visit the Abbey and enjoy the peace and restfulness of the scene.

Fifth day.

ABBOTSFORD AND SELKIRK

Route in brief : Melrose—River Tweed—Darnick—Kaeside —Abbotsford.

Walking distance : 8 miles.

Map : Ordnance Survey 1″ scale, No. 80.

This day you leave Melrose not to return, and as you have only eight miles of walking you are advised to spend the morning exploring the town. After lunch, follow the Tweed-side footpath from the church to the Waverley Hydropathic, at the point on the Tweed called Boatshiel Pool. Turn to the left here, away from the river, past the Hydropathic, to Darnick Tower, one of the once innumerable Border peels.

From Darnick you will follow the by-way leading to Kaeside and out by Shillinglaw Plantation to Bauchlin Cottage, where you turn to the right through the woodlands to come to the house of Abbotsford. You are now in the heart of the romantic country so well described by Sir Walter Scott. Although it is said that he placed the Trossachs on the map for tourists, there is no doubt that he also attracted the attention of his wide circle of readers to this romantic country of the Borders. After enjoying the atmosphere of Abbotsford turn to the left and follow the road alongside the Tweed to the junction of the Tweed and the Ettrick, then follow the Ettrick Water through Lindean and so to Selkirk, which is the end of your day's walking.

Near Selkirk is the Youth Hostel of Broadmeadows, situated on the Yarrow Water. Broadmeadows Hostel has the distinction of being one of the first to be opened in Scotland by the Youth Hostels Association. It consists of a row of four cottages converted into one building on a secluded hill-side looking down the valley of the Yarrow. The ivy-covered ruin at the foot of the garden was the old house of Broad-

meadows which Sir Walter Scott wished to buy. He refers
to it as " the minstrel's lowly bower " in *The Lay*. Not far
from the hostel is the ruin of Newark Castle where, after the
Battle of Phillipheugh, many prisoners were done to death.
Across the valley from Newark Castle is Foulshiels, the
birthplace of Mungo Park.

Although Selkirk is at present given over to the manu-
facture of woollen goods, its principal employment at one
time was the making of shoes.

Sixth day.

THE THREE BRETHREN

Route in brief: Selkirk — Broadmeadows — The Three
Brethren—Glen Kinnon—Ashiesteel—Caddonfoot—Lindean
—Selkirk.

Walking distances: To Clovenfords 9 miles, to Lindean
13 miles, to Selkirk 15 miles.

Map: Ordnance Survey 1″ scale, No. 80.

Cross the River Ettrick to Philiphaugh Farm, where you
find the road leading uphill to the reservoir above the woodlands, at the Long Philip Burn. Beyond the reservoir the
road following along the right-hand side of the stream becomes a track climbing up the valley between Foulshiels Hill
and Peat Law. The higher of these two hills rises to 1,459
feet and where the path you follow leaves the stream, you
have ascended to more than 1,000 feet. The path now makes
an almost direct line towards the summit of the Three Brethren,
but when about 150 feet from the top the main path bears
away to the left to Broomy Law. You will, however, have no
difficulty in finding your way to the summit of the hill.

Should you descend eastwards from the summit of the Three
Brethren you would come to the track leading down to
Yair House, but you are advised to descend to the west,
keeping above the woodlands on the west side of Stony
Knowe. You will then come to the track leading down
Glenkinnon Burn, at the foot of which is Ashiesteel House.
Here Scott lived for ten years, and achieved some of his
earliest successes.

From Ashiesteel House follow the road to the east and

across the River Tweed on to the main road, where you will turn to the right to Caddonfoot and to Clovenfords. Hence you may travel by train through Galashiels back to Selkirk. You can, of course, stay at Clovenfords, but you are recommended to leave your kit at Selkirk and so be free to enjoy the climb over the hills by the Three Brethren. If you feel that to end your walk at Clovenfords is too short a day, you will not cross the River Tweed near Ashiesteel, but instead you follow the by-way on the south side of the Tweed through the woodlands of Yair House and join the main road near Raelees Wood. Here you have an alternative; you can keep to the south side of the river and follow the main road through Ettrickbank back to Philiphaugh, where you cross the river again at Selkirk. The alternative is to cross the River Tweed near Raelees Wood and follow the by-way along the slopes of Rink Hill to join the main road at the point where the Tweed and the Ettrick meet. You then turn right to Lindean Station, where you may end your day's walking and travel by train or bus into Selkirk or complete the round by walking the two miles of main road into Selkirk.

Seventh day.

FASTHEUGH HILL

Route in brief: Selkirk, by-way on left to Ettrick Bridge End—Witchie Knowe—Fastheugh Hill—Newark Hill—Black Andrew Wood—Yarrow Vale—Selkirk.

Walking distance: 18 miles.

Map: Ordnance Survey 1″ scale, No. 80.

The route for to-day, from Selkirk, skirts the deer park and the Haining Loch, beyond which you follow the road to Howden near the junction of the Ettrick and the Yarrow waters. At Howden Farm do not take the by-way curving round towards the river, but turn to the left and, after a further half-mile of walking, you find the track becomes a footpath, leading across the hill to regain the road below Hartwoodmyres. Continue along this road until it joins the riverside road a little more than two miles short of Ettrick Bridge End. In the village itself you cross over the river and should follow along the right-hand bank by the road, when you come to the moorland road leading across from

Yarrow. At the Ettrick Bridge this old road climbs up to a point 1,187 feet above sea-level, where the track bears across to the right up to the Witchie Knowe. At the summit of the hill you leave the track and follow across the moorland to the Black Knowe Head and beyond to the summit of Fauldshope Hill. On the far slopes of this hill you will find a track that leads you to the summit of Fastheugh Hill and then winds away across and down the hill through Black Andrew Wood (also referred to as Blacandro), round by the ruins of Newark Castle to the school at Harewood Glen. Newark Castle, which is well worth a visit, was at one time a royal castle, and was stormed on two occasions by the English.

Be careful, when traversing the moorland, to distinguish the boggy patches. Usually the very marshy parts are identified by the lighter-coloured grass and, in some cases, by the flowering cotton-grass.

The road from the Witchie Knowe across to Fastheugh Hill, is, for most of the way, across the open moorland, and if you do not wish to tackle this country, continue along the drove-road right down to the ford at Yarrow. Here you find a track bearing away to the right to Easter Kershope, beyond which the hill path winds uphill to cross the Craighope Burn and so to the old road winding round the summit of Fastheugh Hill.

Having come to the schoolhouse near Harewood Glen, you continue to the main road on the other side of the river at Bowhill North Lodge, where you have some three miles of walking to Selkirk. When crossing the hill road from the Ettrick to the Yarrow you see on your right the ruin of the peel tower of Kirkhope. Watt o' Harden is said to have lived here during the time when he was courting " The Flower of Yarrow."

Where the road descends to Yarrow you are on the main road connecting Selkirk with St. Mary's Loch. A short distance along the road back to Selkirk you see the remains of Deuchar, from which point the path leads across and through the hills to Traquair (Deuchar-Swire). All the hills and valleys in this region abound in paths and drove-roads and one could well spend a week or a fortnight in the district exploring one section only of these hills. Every glen and every hill holds something in store for you.

Eighth day.

MINCHMOOR

Route in brief: Selkirk—Yarrow Vale—Broadmeadows—Minchmoor Road—Cheese Well—Traquair—Innerleithen.

Walking distance: 13 miles.

Map: Ordnance Survey 1″ scale, No. 80.

Five miles out from Selkirk you come to Yarrow Ford, where the track for Minchmoor Road commences. Here you leave the main road and follow the by-way uphill. On the right-hand side, as you go up the hill, you should have the Gruntly Burn, which comes down the woodland slopes of the Whitehope Rig. Your track, the famous Minchmoor Road, is a well-known drove-road that leads right through the hills to Traquair. When well above the woodlands of Hangingshaw you ascend until you join the drove-road a little to the west of Brown Knowe. This old road you follow across the Minchmoor is a good specimen of the old style of roadmaking—scorning detours and making a direct attack on every obstruction, no matter how formidable and steep. It was the path followed in the retreat from Phillipheugh and, according to an old report, is still used by people who " scorn the luxury of a level but circuitous thoroughfare." An up-to-date writer would re-write this by saying that this old road is much favoured by ramblers.

From the Brown Knowe the track continues to the Hare Law and a little north of Minch Moor (1,856 feet) to the Cheese Well, which is said to have belonged at one time to the fairies. It was an old custom for people when passing to drop in pieces of cheese as offerings to the fairies. Beyond the Cheese Well the track descends, and ere long you find yourself coming to Traquair in the valley approaching the Tweed. The well-known song, " The Bush abune Traquair," was about a grove of birches to the south-west of the village. When you reach the road at Traquair the main part of your walk is finished: it remains only to continue for a further two miles to come to Innerleithen, which is your destination for this day.

Note.—On the fifth, sixth, seventh and eighth days of this tour, the roads given have been within a district well covered by Youth Hostels. If you wished to stay at the Hostels while in this district you would have to modify your excursions somewhat. Particulars of routes and all manner of useful information concerning the Youth Hostel Movement in Scotland will be found in the handbook of the Scottish Youth Hostels Association. This can be obtained from the S.Y.H.A. offices, 451 Lawnmarket, Edinburgh 1.

Ninth day.

THE LEITHEN WATER

Route in brief : Innerleithen—Leithen Water to Craighope Farm—Shieldgreen Farm—Peebles.
Walking distance : 12 miles.
Map : Ordnance Survey 1″ scale, No. 80.

Before leaving Innerleithen you will, of course, visit the St. Ronan's Wells; after having generally explored Innerleithen, follow the road leading up the western bank of the Leithen Water. The road follows along the bottom of a steep valley, on the west side of which is the Lee Pen, and on the east the Pirn Craig and the Kirnie Law. You have about three miles of walking through this glen, and most of the time you are steadily climbing.

For these wanderings through the glens and over the hills you should give particular care to your kit. The clothes you wear should be easy fitting and light, while the rucksack on your back should be large and, as a rule, only half-full. For such a tour as this your rucksack and your kit together should not weigh more than 12 lb. and if you buy a frame rucksack with three pockets outside and three inside you have the equivalent of a fitted suitcase. The wide outside pocket should be for your maps, log-book and drinking-cup; one of the long outside pockets will hold your toilet soap and first-aid necessities; the other outside pocket will be for socks and stockings; the large inside pocket is made to carry clean underwear and so prevent it from becoming mixed up with your sandwiches and slippers. The Bergan type of rucksack is the best to use. The webbing straps are preferable to leather straps, for after a day of very wet weather leather straps become very soft and there is a possibility of a dye coming out on to your clothes.

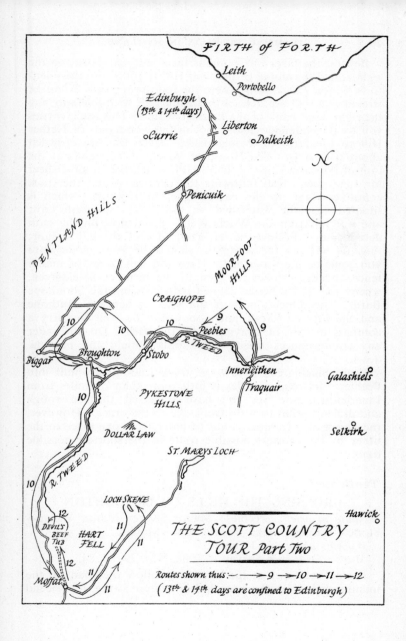

FIRTH OF FORTH

Leith
Portobello

Edinburgh
(13th & 14th days)

Currie

Liberton
Dalkeith

Penicuik

PENTLAND HILLS

MOORFOOT HILLS

CRAIGHOPE

10
10
10 Peebles
9
9

Biggar
Broughton
Stobo
R. TWEED

Innerleithen
Traquair

Galashiels

PYKESTONE HILLS

10

DOLLAR LAW

Selkirk

ST MARYS LOCH

R. TWEED

10

LOCH SKENE

12
DEVIL'S BEEF TUB

HART FELL

11
11

Hawick

THE SCOTT COUNTRY
TOUR Part Two

Moffat

12

11
11

Routes shown thus :— → 9 → 10 → 11 → 12
(13th & 14th days are confined to Edinburgh)

Beyond the farm of Colquhar the road bears away to the right round the slopes of the Dod Hill to follow up the Glentress Water. At a point where the road bears away from the stream you will see a track branching off to the left to hug the right-hand bank of the Leithen Water. This track carries you by the waterside at the foot of the woodlands of Nether Hill to the farm of Woolandslee. Here you are crowded about with hills. The House of Woolandslee stands at the foot of the steep slope of Totto Hill, which rises almost sheer for 1,000 feet. Still following the Leithen Water, the track continues right up the narrow glen to Huthope, which is situated near the watershed on the slopes of Lamb Law, and not far from the Witch Well. From now on the path deteriorates. Follow the left-hand fork of the hill stream; this, as well as the footpath, should be your guide until you come to the watershed. Here you will cross the march fence and drop down the glen to the farm of Shieldgreen, where you find a better defined path crossing the Soonhope Burn. The difficult part of the walk is between Huthope and Shieldgreen Cross, and you would do well to carry a compass in case of straying from the path. Do not under any circumstances attempt this walk should the mist be down.

From Shieldgreen follow the track leading downhill into Peebles. By road, Peebles is little more than six miles from Innerleithen, and yet you have traversed thirteen rough and difficult miles to walk from one to the other. However, the object of a tramper is not to move from one place to the other by the shortest possible route in the shortest possible time.

Tenth day.

CROSSING THE HILLS TO BROUGHTON

Route in brief : Peebles—Manor Sware—Manor Water—Stobo—Hammer Head—Broughton—Moffat.

Walking distance : 12 miles.

Maps : Ordnance Survey 1″ scale, Nos. 79, 80, 84.

From Peebles cross the river and follow the road up the loaning and climb the steep hill of Manor Sware, to descend at once on the other side by a hill just as steep. At the bridge, cross the Manor Water, and turn to the left following the road up the stream as far as the farm of Glack. Here the path continues westward up and over the hill. Before following this path you should visit the Black Dwarf's Cottage. A short distance up the Manor Water road at the Woodhouse Farm, David Ritchie, the Black Dwarf, built a cottage, in which he lived as a recluse. In the churchyard of Manor, where he is buried, Messrs. W. & R. Chambers erected a monument in his memory in 1845. The footpath leads over the hill and down to Easter Dawyck, from which point the track joins the main road near Stobo. Turn to the right on reaching the main road, and at the schoolhouse of Stobo turn to the left, following the hill road that leads upwards to the height and through to Broughton. Here the track keeps to the right-hand side of the Easton Burn, but you should cross at Harrowhope. This track leads you down by the woodlands to the loch at the head of the Weston Burn, but follow the path which continues across the shoulder of the hill and so down to the Hopehead Burn which feeds the loch referred to above. Coming down to the stream the path crosses and then climbs up the other side of the glen on its way to Hammer Head and all the hills beyond; after a while it crosses the junction of two tributaries of the Hopehead Burn, and as this is the last watercourse you will find on this side of the watershed, you are advised to rest here for lunch. After lunch you have a short distance to ascend along the slopes of Hammer Head near the top of the gully when, at the march fence, you come to another path leading from the Tarth Water to the Tweed. Follow this path down by the burn and so to Broughton, whence you travel by bus to Moffat. (Check with local time-tables; at one time the services were three days a week.)

Eleventh day.

THE GREY MARE'S TAIL

Route in brief: Moffat—Moffat Water to a short distance beyond the ninth milestone out of Moffat—Grey Mare's Tail—Loch Skeen—Return same way to Moffat.
Walking distance: 22 miles.
Maps: Ordnance Survey 1″ scale, Nos. 84 and 85.

From Moffat you follow the road to Holmend and the Moffat Water; it entails between nine and ten miles of road walking, but the route is full of interest. A little beyond the second milestone you cross the Craigie Burn and so to the Craigieburn Wood, at the commencement of which is Burns's Cottage. Between the fourth and fifth milestone you pass Shortwoodend. The road steadily climbs until, when you pass the opening of the Blackhope Burn, you are about 600 feet above sea-level. All the way the road follows the winding Moffat Water as it makes its way down the valley at the foot of encompassing hills. Eventually you come to the Grey Mare's Tail in the gully on your left near the watershed. This waterfall leaps over a precipice that is about 80 feet high and almost perpendicular. Some distance below the waterfall the water winds a course through a ravine about 20 feet deep, the walls of which are so straight and narrow that it is almost possible to jump across. This side of the Linn was at one time reputed to be the home of fairies, and at the entrance is what is known as the Elf's Kirk. This was once a cave, but the stone was quarried and so the cave was demolished. From above the Grey Mare's Tail follow the Tail Burn to Loch Skeen, an eerie sheet of water hemmed in by the hills. At one time the wild hills surrounding this rocky basin were a haunt of the eagle, but even a hundred years ago records state that it was very rare to see these birds in the Southern Highlands. One does not like to recommend as a return way the road by which you came, but on this occasion there is no alternative, for it is not advisable to try conclusions with the heights.

Twelfth day.

THE DEVIL'S BEEF TUB

Route in brief : Moffat—By the road to the north along the right-hand side of the Annan Water—Ericstane—Devil's Beef Tub—Auldhouse Hill Bridge—Moffat.

Walking distance : 14 miles.

Map : Ordnance Survey 1" scale, No. 84.

This is the last day of walking in the Scott Country, because on the morrow you journey to Edinburgh. Moffat has been your headquarters for three nights, and on this, the third day, you visit the gully known as the Devil's Beef Tub. This hollow, which is enclosed by hills on three sides is open on the fourth and was used by the Annandale reivers in olden times as a hiding-place for their stolen cattle. Although the name given on the map is the Devil's Beef Tub, the old name for it is the Marquis of Annandale's Beef Stand.

You made your acquaintance with Moffat on the day when you walked from Peebles over the hill. On the second day you visited the Grey Mare's Tail and now you go in a northerly direction along the Annan Water. The Lowther Hills rise up to the west, while to the east is the conglomeration of hills known as the Hartfell Range, culminating in Hart Fell, which is 2,651 feet high. It is not known whether this mountain has grown in the last hundred years, but early in the nineteenth century an authority gave the height as 2,635 feet.

From the town of Moffat, follow the road up to the Moffat Well on the Birnock Water. The town has sometimes been referred to as the " Cheltenham of Scotland," possibly because of its three wells. The one known as the Moffat Well is enclosed in a stone building at the head of the road leading up from Moffat. After visiting the well, retrace your steps to where the road crosses the Hind Gill. Here you will find a track on the right circling round the northern end of the wooded Gallow Hill. This track brings you to the road following the line of the Annan Water where you turn to the right, and follow this valley road for three miles as far as Ericstane Farm. About half a mile before you come to the farm a footpath branches off to Auchincat Burn to what is known as the Hartfell Spa. This spring rises in a ravine on the slopes of Arthur's Seat, which is a southern spur of Hart Fell. At Ericstane Farm a track continues to Corehead Farm, where a footpath leads to the side of the Devil's Beef Tub round the shoulder of Great Hill. Immediately above the woodlands of Corehead, bear to the left across the mouth of the Beef Tub to the road at a point marked on the map as Eric Stane. Turn to the right here, and on this side of the first milestone follow the track on the right to Tweed's Well which marks the source of the River Tweed. In this short walk from the road you have crossed into Lanarkshire. From the Tweed's Well you have a short walk to the road where, by turning to the left, you are faced with a walk of eight and a half miles to Moffat. When you come to the milestone that reads " 44 miles to Edinburgh " you will be at the point where the counties of Dumfriesshire, Peeblesshire and Lanarkshire meet. Little more need be said about the return journey to Moffat, but you will find every minute of the three hours needed for this part of the walk full of interest.

Over the hill to the west is a valley through which the railway sweeps down from Beattock. Whoever has travelled this way remembers the pull of the train to the summit and the sense of gathering speed as the train races down from Beattock to the border.

Following the road down the eastern side of the Annan Water you come once again to Moffat and so to the end of your excursion.

Thirteenth and Fourteenth days.
EDINBURGH

Route in brief: Bus from Moffat to Edinburgh, or train from Beattock to Edinburgh.

This is not a day of walking but a day of sightseeing. You are recommended to climb Arthur's Seat and visit the many places of historic and romantic interest in the city. As there is no walking on this day it is not necessary to obtain a large-scale map; however, if you are keen to get this particular map it is No. 74 in the 1-inch-to-the-mile series of the

Robert M. Adam

FAST CASTLE

KIRKCUDBRIGHT

Ordnance Survey. The large-scale map of the city can be obtained from the Edinburgh tramway offices. Edinburgh is not a city that can be " done " in a few minutes. Therefore it is considered worth while to devote two days to exploring Edinburgh, but should you feel that you have had enough of the city streets after one day, you should spend the last day of your holiday visiting the Pentland Hills, doing the excursion given for the second day in the Forth and Clyde Tour.

II

GALLOWAY

INTRODUCTION

THE south-west corner of Scotland contains some of the wildest and loveliest of districts with enough scenery to occupy many weeks of holiday, especially a walking tour. In fact it is quite a difficult matter to plan a tour for two weeks because there is so much from which to choose. It was decided, therefore, to select one district, and the one chosen is Galloway. Much had to be omitted, but at the same time much has been included, and at the end of the tour you may feel satisfied that you have had in full measure one which is comprehensive and which includes the various kinds of country and seaside the south-west has to offer.

You start at Dumfries, so closely associated with Burns, and, after a visit to Sweetheart Abbey, climb Criffell for a far-flung view over Scotland and England. Then through the Stewartry of Kirkcudbright to the Shire and over the Machers to finish up by exploring the little-known, out-of-the-way places of the Rinns of Galloway. You will see smugglers' caves and smugglers' harbours, hear tell of the Covenanters and of Mary, Queen of Scots. If you want to read stories of the district you should get *Highways and Byways in Galloway and Carrick*, by the Rev. C. H. Dick.

Other books to read which deal with parts of the country through which you travel are *The Thirty-Nine Steps*, by John Buchan, and *Guy Mannering*, by Sir Walter Scott. Dorothy L. Sayers in her *Four Red Herrings* uses some of the roads you will follow. The wildest part of the tour will be round about Gatehouse of Fleet and Creetown. After that you have a much more peaceful scene, especially when following the line of Luce Bay and, later, when wandering through the

country of the Rinns. While there is an air of remoteness
the outlook is gentle and so much less forbidding than those
stern and barren lands north of Gatehouse.

First day.

Travel by train to Dumfries.

Second day.

SWEETHEART ABBEY AND CRIFFELL

Route in brief : Dumfries—Lochanhead—Lochaber Loch—
Whinnyhill — Sweetheart Abbey — Criffell — Mainsriddle —
Dalbeattie.

Walking distance : 15 miles.

Maps : Ordnance survey 1″ scale, Nos. 88 and 92.

The chief glories past and present of Dumfries are Burns
and the River Nith. There are many memorials to the national
bard, but the Globe Inn has been referred to as " the temple
to the conviviality of Burns where drinkers have kept alight
an alcoholic enthusiasm for generations." The poet's chair
at the inn comes in for special attention from the visitor and
is " protected from the unworthy posteriors of this earth "
by a wooden bar.

The River Nith is spanned at one point in Dumfries by the
Dervorgilla Bridge (built by the inhabitants of Dumfries in
1432) where each of the six arches makes a frame for the
cameo of the smiling river. Travel on the Dalbeattie bus as
far as Lochanhead; continue along the main road for a short
distance farther to Moorend, where you turn left along the
track to Lochaber Loch, and on, past the fifteen tons of the
Rocking Stone, to the main Kirkbean road near Whinnyhill.
If you look at your map you see, just north of the hill, a place
called Constantinople, and not so very far away to the south
is Shambellie.

When joining the main road, turn to the right and you come
to the village of New Abbey, and the ruins of Sweetheart
Abbey which was saved from the hands of a quarry-master
by the payment of £40 by some local folk.

Sweetheart Abbey is associated with a delightful story that
concerns John Balliol and Dervorgilla; part of that story is

told by H. V. Morton, while a more prosaic rendering is given in the *Imperial Gazetteer of Scotland*.

Continue southwards along the Kirkbean road as far as Drumburn, where the ascent of Criffell commences. With the aid of your map the summit is reached without difficulty. Criffell (1,766 feet) is the dominating height in the district and the expansive view of sea and land is most impressive. You see Loch Kindar near at hand, most of the Solway, much of England and a great deal of Scotland.

Cross the hills by way of Boreland Hill, Craigtappock and Airdrie Hill and then descend to Mainsriddle. From here travel by bus to Dalbeattie.

Third day.

SOUTH TO DUNDRENNAN

Route in brief : Dalbeattie—Gelston—Bentuder—Hass—Blackbreast—Fellcroft Loch—Dundrennan.

Walking distance : 16 miles.

Map : Ordnance Survey 1″ scale, No. 92.

Out from Dalbeattie on the Castle Douglas road you come to the bridge across the Urr, and up the hill beyond the river are the quarries of Craignair, the granite of which has been sent to many parts of the world. The lower part of Eddystone Lighthouse is built of Craignair granite and the stone for two lighthouses in far Ceylon was quarried here. Near the Buittle bridge is Buittle church and also the site of the castle. Something of their story is told by the Rev. C. H. Dick in his *Highways and By-ways of Galloway and Carrick*.

It is suggested that you commence this excursion by hitch-hiking as far as the smithy at the cross-roads just beyond the Buittle road-end (the service bus to Castle Douglas goes direct by the Buittle route). Begin your walk by following the road to Gelston and continue beyond the village for two and a half miles along the Kirkcudbright road. Then turn to the left to Castlehill farm, but keep to the path which starts at Over Linkins and takes you over the hills to the hill road at Hass *via* Bentuder. Carry on by way of Blackbreast and Fell-croft Loch down to the road at East Kirkcarswell. From the cottage of Hass you traverse the open hill and go over and

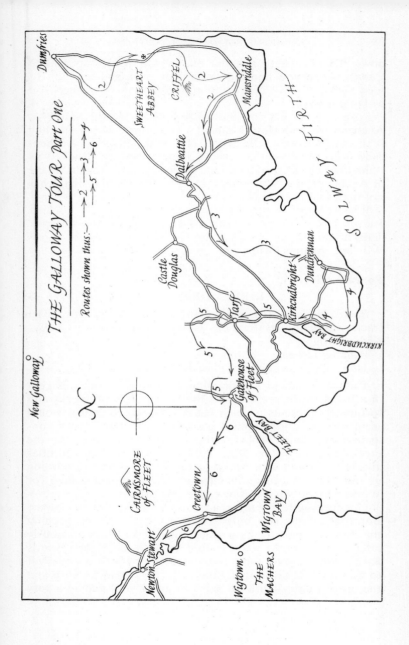

THE GALLOWAY TOUR part one

Routes shown thus:—
2 → 3 →
5 → 6 →

New Galloway

N

Dumfries

SWEETHEART ABBEY

CRIFFEL

Mainsriddle

Dalbeattie

Castle Douglas

Tarff

Kirkcudbright

Dundrennan

SOLWAY FIRTH

KIRKCUDBRIGHT BAY

Gatehouse of Fleet

FLEET BAY

CAIRNSMORE OF FLEET

Creetown

WIGTOWN BAY

Newton Stewart

Wigtown

THE MACHERS

down Blackbreast to a house marked on your map as The Cabin, where you find a moorland track that leads you to East Kirkcarswell, whence a more substantial road brings you to Dundrennan.

From the heights you should be able to see the Solway— Auchencairn and Heston Island. Contained within the bay is the smaller one of Balcary. The small village of Auchencairn runs down to the sea and is described by Crockett as " the little bright rose-bowered, garden-circled, seaside village of Auchencairn." Certainly it can be said that the village has not been built to any plan.

What a lot of interesting names the map shows ! Look at Heston Island. What is behind the name Daft Ann's Steps ? Then across on the mainland are the following names : Lot's Wife and Adam's Chair.

Fourth day.

KIRKCUDBRIGHT

Route in brief : Dundrennan—Abbey Burnfoot—Coast track *via* Dirk Hatteraick Cove — Kirkcudbright Bay— Kirkcudbright.

Walking distance : 12 miles.

Map : Ordnance Survey 1″ scale, No. 92.

The old Abbey of Dundrennan, long since in ruins, is kept in a fine state of preservation by the Ministry of Works and fortunately presents a much better appearance than it would seem to have done about a hundred years ago when a contemporary writer deplored the neglected condition of the precincts. The history of the Abbey goes back many centuries and is connected with Mary, Queen of Scots who, according to the story, stayed at Dundrennan prior to embarking for Workington at what is now called Port Mary.

Go due south, by the road from Dundrennan, to Abbey Burnfoot, about two miles away. A little before reaching the coast you pass the by-way leading to Port Mary previously referred to. At Abbey Burnfoot turn to the right towards Kirkcudbright, but turn at the second by-way on the left to go *via* Corrahill to the Dunrod Burn. Cross the burn and the open country (with no paths to guide you) and in a very

short time you come to a little-used track at a house marked
on the map as Howwell. Keep going in a westerly direction
and at Little Balmae turn towards the coast, but where the
track ends go westwards again to join a coastline track that
starts at Dirk Hatteraick Cove and goes all the way to Kirkcudbright. This coastline walk gives you an uninterrupted
view of Kirkcudbright Bay and across to the western end of
the bay where the hill of Meikle Ross stands guard with the
island of Little Ross as an outpost. (*Note.*—At the time of
writing the route described in the preceding paragraph is
closed to the public, but it is hoped to reopen it shortly.)
The river flows into Kirkcudbright Bay and at the estuary
you have wide stretches of sand at low tide.

The map again discloses many peculiar place names worthy
of following up—Manxman's Lake, Paul Jones Point, French-
man's Rock and Devil's Threshing Floor.

Fifth day.

KIRKCONNELL

Route in brief : Train to Tarff—Barcaple—Meadowpark—
Kirkconnell — Pharaoh's Throne — Trostrie — Drumwall —
Gatehouse of Fleet.

Walking distance : 14 miles.

Map : Ordnance Survey 1″ scale, No. 92.

What is " sleech " ?   Apparently Kirkcudbright is surrounded with it at low tide. Lord Cockburn in his *Current
Journeys* says that " at low tide the town is surrounded by a
world of ' sleech ' and that it looks like a town surrounded
by a lake of bird lime." That is not all. Defoe wrote of the
place as a " harbour without ships, a port without trade, and
a fishery without nets." The place has been called at high
tide the Venice of Scotland, and so why not call it the place
of the mud and the flood ?

Travel by train to Tarff and start walking there. Turn to
the left at the station, and then to the right at the cross-roads
and follow this road northwards by Barcaple and Fellend to
Meadowpark. Here turn left along the track across Kirkconnell and pass the Martyrs' Monument to reach the stream
which flows out of Loch Mannoch. Do not cross the stream

but follow alongside it for a short distance until you come to the path that takes you in a southerly direction over Pharaoh's Throne to the road at Trostrie. Here you have crossed a moorland closely linked with the Covenanters, and the monument on the moor is a reminder and a link with their story. Go south from Trostrie along the road, but only to the first turning on the right, where another moorland track which originally was a military road takes you eastward to Gatehouse of Fleet. This old military highway crosses Irelandtown Moor with an altitude of never more than 650 feet. Gatehouse is near the estuary of the Water of Fleet and the district between here and Creetown is the country of *Guy Mannering* with Kippletringan as the covering name for Gatehouse.

An alternative route is to break away from the direction already described when on Kirkconnell Moor. Instead of going south over Pharaoh's Throne, continue westward over Fuffock Hill and Cairntosh Hill down to Gatehouse.

Sixth day.

THE CORSE OF SLAKES

Route in brief: Gatehouse of Fleet—Anwoth—Corse of Slakes Road—Creetown—Lennies—Newton Stewart.

Walking distance: 11 miles.

Maps: Ordnance Survey 1″ scale, Nos. 91 and 87.

The district between Gatehouse of Fleet and Creetown is full of interest and offers more than one tramping excursion. Some will advise you to go round by the coast and explore Dirk Hatteraick Cave at Kirkdale Glen; others will say that you should go northwards, and then westwards from Gatehouse in order to enjoy the contrast between the placid loveliness of the lands of Gatehouse with the stark barrenness of arid moorlands a few miles north. Only one route can be taken for the latter excursion and this will be almost due west by the old military road over the Corse of Slakes.

Leave the town by the Fleet bridge and turn right to the Manse, but before reaching that house turn to the left along a footpath to Anwoth, but look out for, and do not miss seeing, Cardoness Castle. You should also see the monument to Samuel Rutherford, long ago a minister of Anwoth; it stands on the crest of a nearby hill. From here you walk along the old military road called the Corse of Slakes, a name supposed to mean " the crossing of the passes." Almost at once you start climbing and in a short time you have ascended 300 feet (the highest point on the road is a little under 900 feet). Then comes the descent to the Balloch Burn, and so to Creetown (Port an Ferry in *Guy Mannering*) where you join a road coming down by the Moneypool Burn (referred to in the *Five Red Herrings*, by Dorothy L. Sayers). When descending from the summit of the Corse of Slakes Road you should see the Druids' Circle, which is on the left as you approach the bridge over the Englishman's Burn.

Newton Stewart is your destination, and the only way to reach it is by the main road. The distance is between five and six miles and, since the walk is of no particular interest, you are advised to make use of either the train or the bus. You have followed the line of the River Cree in coming to Newton Stewart, a river which acts as a boundary between the Shire and the Stewartry. The Hill of Cairnsmore rises behind the town with its two attendant villages of Creebridge and Minnigaff. The general scene, according to one writer, is " much like the face of Switzerland."

Seventh day.

REST DAY

The first six days of the holiday have not called for any particularly strenuous walks but, nevertheless, it will be good to have an easy day. If you feel like relaxing with a book you should read *Guy Mannering* or John Buchan's *Thirty-nine Steps*, which also refers to this district.

If you want an easy afternoon ramble, visit Garlies Castle on the north side of Cumloden Deer Park. You go northwards from Newton Stewart to Kirkland, and then cross the Penkiln Burn at Cumloden and so by the path through Garlies Wood to the Castle.

A longer walk of about eleven miles is to Bargaly Glen and back by the old Edinburgh road. Travel by bus or train to Palnure, the first stop on the Creetown route, and start walking by following the Palnure Burn right up through Bargaly Glen to come out on the road at Talnotry cottage. This involves about five miles of walking. For the return journey cross the moor from Talnotry cottage for a short distance to a lochan shown on the map as the Loch of the Lowes. The track of the old Edinburgh road skirts the loch, a track which you will follow until you join the main road. The road is clear to Newton Stewart, giving you a round walk of about eleven miles.

To-morrow you will continue west towards Stranraer, but you will be tempted to go north to the region of utter wildness where Loch Trool is cradled, and where the five hills of Merrick —" the five fingers of the awful hand "—dominate the scene. If you would know Galloway more fully you must come many times; there is so much to see, there are so many places to be visited, that many which you feel must be seen have to be left for another tour. The long road north out of Newton Stewart takes you to a particularly interesting region of Galloway—a region that excels in wildness and loveliness any part of the Highlands of Scotland.

Eighth day.

THE MACHERS

Route in brief: Newton Stewart—Glenluce Road—Low Knockbrex—Wigtown Road—Clugston Loch—Craigeach Fell —Challochglass Moor—Whitefield Loch—Glenluce.
Walking distance: 12 miles.
Maps: Ordnance Survey 1″ scale, Nos. 87, 91 and 90.

Leave Newton Stewart by the main Glenluce road but, a mile out, turn left to go south along a by-way that stretches out for about four or five miles to join the main Wigtown highway. You leave the Newton Stewart-Glenluce road at Knockbrex, then at the main Wigtown road turn to the right and very soon you cross the River Bladnoch and then turn left at Spittal. About a mile from the turning you come to the small Clugston Loch and, at the bend in the road, you see a track that skirts the north end of the loch and then bears westwards; this track keeps to the northern slopes of Craigeach Fell, the highest point ahead of you. Soon afterwards

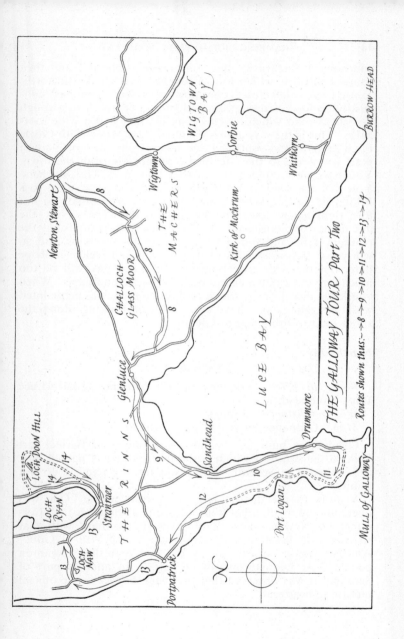

THE GALLOWAY TOUR Part Two

Routes shown thus:— →8 →9 →10 →11 →12 →13 →14

LOCH DOON HILL

LOCH RYAN

LOCH NAW

Stranraer

THE RINNS

Portpatrick

Port Logan

Drummore

MULL OF GALLOWAY

Newton Stewart

CHALLOCH GLASS MOOR

Glenluce

THE MACHERS

Wigtown

Kirk of Mochrum

Sorbie

Whithorn

WIGTOWN BAY

LUCE BAY

Sandhead

BURROW HEAD

N

you come to a farm of the same name as the hill and then comes Fell Loch, which you see just before reaching the north-south road.   The track continues westwards and has sufficiently improved to be promoted from a footpath to a rough moorland road which, in effect, means that it is a wide footpath.   This is the way across Challochglass Moor, with Castle Loch seen to the south.   Four miles from the north-south road you come to the Glenluce road not far from the town. You have now crossed the district known as The Machers. You join the road at Machermore, and almost at once pass Whitefield Loch.   When you come to the cross-roads do not turn right but go ahead to the coast at the Crow's Nest, the old name for Stairhaven on Luce Bay.   Borrow visited the place in 1866 and found it very much to his liking and so will you.   If you have a camera you will find plenty of scope here, but the wide, sweeping view of Luce Bay will be too much for your camera except perhaps for a cloudscape.   When you leave the old pier, which in days gone by was acquainted with smuggling, you have two miles of walking along the shore road to bring you to Glenluce.

Ninth day.

LUCE BAY

Route in brief: Glenluce—Main Stranraer road—Luce Bay—Sandhead.

Walking distance : 9 miles.

Map : Ordnance Survey 1″ scale, No. 90.

Glenluce is built on the north-west slope of Barlockhart Fell, to the south of which is the most strangely named hill; it is called The Several—the reason for the name I do not know.

Visitors to the district react in various ways.   One was overcome by the Sunday (that was quite a while ago).   " Certainly no Nation on earth observes the Sabbath with that strictness of devotion and resignation to the Will of God." Another visitor was struck by the fact that the " common people wear bonnets instead of hats."   In another part of Scotland it was observed that the black bowler is the official mourning headgear.

Leaving Glenluce, which is supposed to be famous for its devil and its abbey, go along the Stranraer road for a little over two miles and then, after passing the house of White-crook on your right, take the turning on the left just short of where the railway crosses over the main road and follow the curve of Luce Bay all the way to Sandhead. Given a day of sunshine, you have a shining sea as your companion all the day and at the end of your journey you will sleep within sound of the sea. The Bay of Luce is the southernmost in Scotland, and at low tide a wide belt of sand is left uncovered. The bay and Loch Ryan have eaten into the land south and north, leaving a hammer-shaped promontory called The Rinns which is the western of the three districts of Wigtownshire.

Sandhead seems to have little or no story; its bay is a small natural harbour, but not for ships of any size. Even the *Gazetteer* can say no more than that there is an inn, a school and a post office. There are no great heights in this district, which is farther south than any other part of Scotland.

Tenth day.

THE RINNS

Route in brief : Sandhead—Ardwell—Chapel Rossan—Laggan Mills—Portacree—Balgown—Terally Bay—Kilstay Bay—Drummore.

Walking distance : 10 miles.

Map : Ordnance Survey 1″ scale, No. 90.

You have ten miles of coastline to follow to-day and there is a main road all the way so there is no need to give directions. Instead, it will be best to talk of places seen by the way or near-at-hand. About a mile out from Sandhead is the old church of Kirkmadrine, of particular interest to the antiquarian.

Continuing south, and keeping close to the shore all the way, you pass Drumantrae Bay to come to the placid village of Ardwell. In all the districts of the Rinns there are no railways except the one connecting from the east to Stranraer. The road coach is still the conveyance, but now it is a motor-coach instead of a horse-drawn coach. Just before entering

Ardwell village you pass Murder Plantation, while not very far away is Bones Plantation; the latter is marked on the 1-inch Ordnance Survey map but not the former. Within the first-named plantation is a gravestone with the word " Murder " engraved on it. Here a McDougall, murdered in the sixteenth century, was buried.

A little south of Ardwell a deviation nearer the coastline is possible. Leave the main road at Chapel Rossan and re-join at Balgown. The climate of this district is so mild that even palm trees grow in the open. These trees can also be seen growing out-of-doors in other parts of Scotland—Arran, for example.

The rest of the route is by way of a series of bays—Terally, Kilstay and, finally, Drummore Bay, your destination for the night.

Eleventh day.

THE MULL OF GALLOWAY

Route in brief : Drummore—Damnaglaur—Mull of Gallo-way—East and Mid Muntloch—Barncorkrie Moor—Clanyard Bay—Port Logan.

Walking distance : 15 miles.

Map : Ordnance Survey 1″ scale, No. 90.

You go south by the road which ends at the lighthouse on Gallie Craig, the most southerly point in Scotland, where you can see the Isle of Man and also the coast of Ireland. In fact the Isle of Man is only 22½ miles away in a direct line, and Ireland not more than 26 miles. In East Tarbet Bay (on Luce Bay and quite near the Mull) is a small cave called The Chapel, or St. Medan's Cave, and near by are the Wells of the Co'. The superstitious folk were wont to gather here on the first Sunday in May and bathe in these natural cavities and leave gifts in the caves and, by so doing, hoped to be cured of their ailments. The story goes on to say that the rest of the day was spent in " gossiping and amusements."

Near the lighthouse you cross the remains of old Pictish fortifications, where the last of the Picts are supposed to have dug themselves in. From the Mull of Galloway you return, by the way you came, back to the road fork, where you turn west to East and Mid Muntlock and Auchneight where a road brings you near the coastline at Slockmill, whence a better road takes you to High Clanyard over Barncorkrie Moor. You are not far from the coast here, but to obtain an idea of the magnificent rocks it is necessary to go by boat from Clanyard Bay round by Laggantalluch Head—the finest scene of its kind around the coast of Scotland.

From Clanyard, continue by the coast track all the way to Port Logan, where there is a sandy bay. At one point of your walk northwards you are very near the coast—Crammag Head—and from there for some time, going north, you have an uninterrupted view out to sea.

Twelfth day.

THE FISH POND

Route in brief : Port Logan—Fish Pond—Salt Pans—Ringuinea—Meikle Float—Portpatrick.
Walking distance : 12 miles.
Map : Ordnance Survey 1″ scale, No. 90.

Only one rest day has been given in this tour and that is in the first week. It is felt there is no need for a rest day in the second week because you are moving on in easy stages, each day doing an average of ten or twelve miles.

Round the bay, from the village of Port Logan, is the Fish Pond, where the fish eat out of your hand. The pond is a natural basin filled by tides and is usually crowded with fish that become so tame that they will rise and take food offered to them. It has been said that fish have been lifted out of the water, stroked and put back again. Similar scenes are enacted at the fish ponds of a hatchery in Stirlingshire, where the fish will jump out of the water on the approach of the man with the bucket of food scraps.

The destination to-day is Portpatrick, and so, all day, you go northwards following the roads and tracks that will keep you as near as possible to the coastline. From the Fish Pond, go by the road *via* Mount Sallie to Port Gill and on to the Salt Pans (check this with your map). Next you come to Float Bay and Ringuinea. Climb up from the bay to Little Float to follow the high road inland from the sea until you come to a triangular meeting of roadways. Go to the left by the Port of Spittal, and continue to Portpatrick. Here and there are one or two conflicting by-ways, but if you study your maps as you go and are guided by them you should not find yourself in any difficulties.

Thirteenth day.

LOCHNAW

Route in brief: Portpatrick—Reservoirs—Loch Naw—Leswalt—Craigencross—Loch Ryan—Stranraer.
Walking distance: 14 miles.
Map: Ordnance Survey 1″ scale, No. 90.

About half a mile out from Portpatrick is the Castle of Dunskey perched on a rocky height above the sea. There is a gully on either side of the rock and from one side you have a particularly impressive view of the height and the steepness of the rocks. A little north of the town is the bay of Port Mara and here, on the south side, is a cave known as the Cave of Ouchtriemackain. The tradition attached to this place is similar to the Wells of the Co' at the Mull of Galloway. The story-teller says that people visit the cave on the first night in May and that at a spring in the cave diseased children are washed in the hope that there may be a miraculous cure.

Cross the golf-links from Portpatrick and then go by the road that passes near Dunskey House, after which you turn to the left to the house marked as Ouchtriemackain. A footpath starts here and goes across to Killantringan, where a farm road to the right, and away from the sea, connects with the road. Turn to the left here and in less than two miles the road forks. The right-hand way is to Stranraer, but go along the left-hand branch of the road up to where it joins a highway at right angles. Go to the right, to come, almost at once, to Loch Naw which is on the south side of the road. The present Castle of Lochnaw is on the south side of the loch but the old castle (what is left of it) is on the island in the loch. A one-time owner of the estate drained the loch and used much of the material from the castle for other purposes.

Beyond the loch the road goes through Aldouran Glen to

LUCE BAY

Robert M. Adam

LOCH NAW

Leswalt, near the shores of Loch Ryan, whence, by turning to the right, a final walk of a little over three miles ends the day at Stranraer.

Fourteenth day.

LOCH DOON HILL

Route in brief: Stranraer—Loch Ryan—Claddy House Burn—Loch Doon Hill—Awies—Braid Fell—Stranraer.

Walking distance: 13 miles.

Map: Ordnance Survey 1″ scale, No. 90.

If you wish to include a rest day in the second week of the tour you could exclude this walk to Loch Doon Hill, which would then enable you to finish at Stranraer. The walk to Loch Doon Hill and back is certainly worth while, but if you leave it out you can still say you have accomplished quite a comprehensive tour of Galloway.

The first part of the walk takes you along the road that skirts the eastern side of Loch Ryan. Continue along this road for about five miles until you come to Claddy House. Here, turn to the right and follow the path up the Claddy House Burn. This turning is about a mile short of Cairnryan. You pass a school at Claddy House and then, after crossing the burn, you find a track leading up the glen from the right of the road. Keep to the north side of the glen for about a mile, and then the path crosses the stream, deteriorates, but takes you round the north side of Loch Doon Hill where you see the small Loch Ree on your left. You then turn south at a point marked Awies on the map, and the track takes you southwards, between Loch Doon Hill and Diddles Hill, across Braid Fell down to the road at Kirklachie Burn. Very soon you come to the lochside road, where two miles of walking brings you back to Stranraer and the end of the tour. You will be surprised at your total mileage and would be even more surprised if you wrote a list of the lochs seen, and hills, big and little, climbed. If you have used your camera during the tour you are going to have some interesting nights in the coming winter reliving the days spent in the summer in Galloway.

4

III

THE NATIONAL FOREST PARK, ARGYLL

THE Argyll National Forest Park is situated in the county of Argyll on the lands of Ardgarten, Glenfinart, Benmore and Glenbranter. On March 12, 1935, the Forestry Commission appointed a National Forest Park committee to advise how the surplus and unplantable land in the forests of the districts referred to might be put to public use.

These estates, which are divided into two main blocks, comprise nearly a hundred square miles and include more than forty mountains, the highest of which is Beinn Ime (3,318 feet), higher than Ben Lomond. One block of the estate commences at Strone Point (dividing the Holy Loch and Loch Long) and from this point the eastern boundary is Loch Long as far as Carrick, just round the bend in Loch Goil. From here the march strikes uphill and along a line of heights almost to Strachur where it crosses the main road to include Beinn Mhòr, west of Loch Eck, and so over the hills to Glen Massan and the Holy Loch.

The other and smaller block comprising the Ardgarten and Ardgoil estates is bounded by the northern shores of Loch Goil and the western shores of Loch Long. This area includes The Cobbler and Beinn Ime, whence the northern march continues to Glen Kinglas and then *via* Loch Restil and The Rest and be Thankful to Lochgoilhead.

At Lochgoilhead is situated the Highland Park of the Glasgow Corporation, an area which adds a further acreage to that of the National Forest Park. The Benmore estate belonged originally to Mr. H. G. Younger who, in 1925, presented the house and grounds to the Forestry Commission.

The committee has issued a Guide to the Argyll National

Forest Park, copies of which can be obtained from The Forestry Commission, 9 Savile Row, London, W.1, or 25 Drumsheugh Gardens, Edinburgh, 3. In the foreword to the first edition the chairman of the Forestry Commission said: " The purpose of the Argyll National Forest Park is primarily to provide recreational facilities for those who love the Scottish mountains, forests and lochs."

The following is a list of the principal heights in the area:

	Feet		Feet
Beinn Ime	3,318	Cnoc na Tricriche ..	1,986
Beinn Narnain ..	3,036	Sligrachan Hill ..	1,805
The Cobbler ..	2,890	Stronchullin Hill ..	1,798
Beinn Luibhean ..	2,811	Creachan Beag ..	1,792
A'Chrois	2,785	Meall Reamhar ..	1,708
Ben Donich ..	2,774	The Saddle	1,704
The Brack	2,580	Carn Glas	1,648
Beinn Bheula .	2,557	Meall Breac ..	1,583
Cnoc Coinnich ..	2,497	A'Chruach	1,570
Beinn Mhòr ..	2,433	Tom a Bhiorain ..	1,561
Beinn Ruadh ..	2,178	Am Binnein ..	1,560
Creachan Mòr ..	2,156	Cnoc a' Mhadaidh ..	1,542
Sgùrr a' Choinnich ..	2,148	Beinn Lagan ..	1,526
Beinn Reithe ..	2,141	Castle Craig ..	1,484
Beinn Dubhain ..	2,114	Meall Dubh ..	1,428
Clach Bheinn ..	2,109	Blairmore Hill ..	1,402
Cruach a' Bhuic ..	2,084	Tom nan Gamhna	1,266
Carnach Mor ..	2,079	The Steeple	1,257
Cruach a' Chaise ..	2,069	Tom Molach ..	1,210
Beinn Bhreac ..	2,043	Cnap Rheamhar ..	1,087
Beinn Bheag ..	2,029	Tom Soillier ..	905

This chapter cannot possibly be considered a comprehensive survey of all that the Park has to offer. All that can be done is to give a very brief sketch and then guide the reader to the principal tramping grounds.

The area is well served with hostels—Whistlefield, Strone, Ardgarten and Glen Loin. No doubt there will be further developments in the next few years but it is not possible here to venture a forecast.

Forest Information

The trampers' playground in the Forest Park is above the timber-line, and it is not intended that members of the public shall have free access to the planted areas. Instead, marked access paths have been, or will be, planned to lead from public roads, through planted areas, to the open hill-side.

Access path-markers are wooden posts painted black and marked with a white arrow. Trampers following these paths should not use the posts for firewood. It has been known !

All these planted areas in the Forest Park, except the access paths, are " out of bounds " and, according to the by-laws covered by the 1927 Forestry Act, it is a punishable offence to trespass, light a fire, smoke a cigarette, strike a light or use a cigarette lighter. It is an equally punishable offence to deposit litter (including dead animals).

The fire hazard is a very real one and is the biggest headache to all who work in the forest. The greatest danger period is from February to May, but once the new grass is through, the hazard is not so great. Some access paths are closed during this danger period.

First day.

Travel to Dunoon.

Travel by train and boat from Glasgow (Central) *via* Gourock, or from Glasgow (Queen St.) *via* Craigendoran to Dunoon. If it is your intention to use the hostels of the Scottish Youth Hostel Association you stay at Whistlefield on Loch Eck side or at Strone. Buses leave from Dunoon, almost at the entrance to the pier; there is a frequent service to Strone on the Ardentinny service and a not so frequent service to Whistlefield on the route to Strachur. If the Strachur service does not fit in with your arrival then travel by the Ardentinny bus as far as the Eachaig Bridge and walk from there to the hostel.

If it is your intention to use the hostels during the whole tour, check up beforehand with the up-to-date issue of the *S.Y.H.A. Handbook* because there may be hostel changes from time to time. Do not forget to book in advance for the hostels.

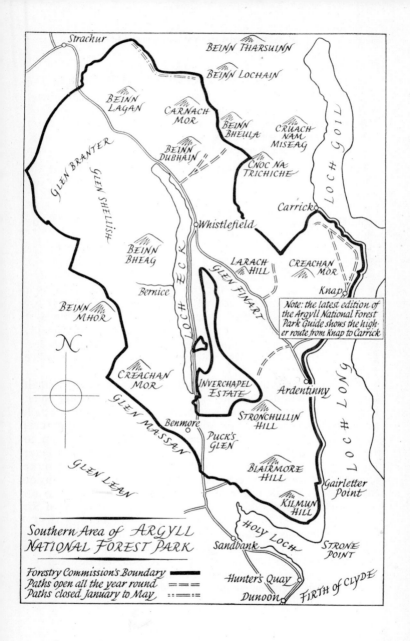

Southern Area of ARGYLL
NATIONAL FOREST PARK

Forestry Commission's Boundary ▬▬▬
Paths open all the year round ═══
Paths closed January to May ≕≕≕

Second day.

PUCK'S GLEN AND BENMORE NURSERIES

Route in brief : Follow the main road from either hostel to the glen and Benmore House in Strath Eachaig.

Walking distance : 5 miles from either hostel.

Map : Ordnance Survey 1″ scale, No. 65, or special map, " Rothesay and the Firth of Clyde."

The entrances to Benmore House and to Puck's Glen are situated in Strath Eachaig on the main road between the Eachaig Bridge, at the head of the Holy Loch, and Loch Eck. The entrance to the glen is on the east side of the main road, while the Benmore House gates are on the other side of the road, about half a mile nearer Loch Eck.

Since Benmore House and grounds were presented to the Forestry Commission in 1925 by Mr. H. G. Younger, the grounds have been utilised as a forest nursery and the house, as well as being the office for the Benmore Forest area, is a forest training centre for apprentice foresters. The course for the young foresters is of two years' duration. The grounds of Benmore House, which contain many botanical specimens, are open to the public upon payment of an admission fee. Times of admission can be obtained from the Forestry Office (telephone, Sandbank 201).

Puck's Glen Arboretum in Strath Eachaig occupies a small section of the hill-side and was opened to the public some years ago. There is nothing artificial except the paths, which have been planned with exquisite taste and made as natural as possible. The path from the main entrance leads up to the House of Puck—a little wooden building where Peter Pan ought to live and where Snow White would be quite at home. There are two inscriptions on the walls inside the house. The one above the fireplace reads: " This hut and glen are dedicated by his friends to the memory of Sir Isaac Bayley Balfour in fulfilment of a plan he cherished." The other notice reads: " Remember James Duncan who had the foresight and courage to originate the planting which clothed these hills and glens with the woods you now enjoy." (Mr. Duncan was the owner of the estate before Mr. Younger.)

There are eighteen named wooden panels in this forest

house representing the various species of timber grown on the estate.

Weymouth Pine	Nobel Fir
Monterey Pine	Thuia
Scots Pine	Corsican Pine
Poplar	Douglas Fir
Cryptomeria (Japonica)	Caucasian Fir
Western Hemlock	Wellingtonia
European Larch	Sitka Spruce
Norway Spruce	Oak
Monkey Puzzle	Lawson Cypress

Some splendid specimens of the giant Sequoia—the *Wellingtonia*—are growing in the glen and fringe the road in the Strath. These giants, indigenous to North America, immortalise the memory of the Sequoyah Indians, protectors of the forest.

Beyond the House of Puck the track continues to still higher ground and then returns by the side of the burn to the road. This path, which in autumn is covered by a rich russet carpet of Thuya twigs, descends the steep glen in company with the hill stream and at times curves round deep dark pools where you have an almost irresistible impulse to drop stones into the deep waters and listen for the " plonk."

Third day.

BEINN MHÒR RANGE

Access : Public road through Glen Massan. Proposed Forestry Commission access path from Loch Eck side up Bernice Glen to Bernice Gap. Proposed access path up Glen Shellish from Bridgend at the north end of Loch Eck.

Map : Ordnance Survey 1″ scale, No. 65, or special map, " Rothesay and the Firth of Clyde."

Hostels : Whistlefield and Strone.

This range of hills in the National Forest Park is situated to the west of Loch Eck. To the north the boundary is Glen Shellish and Glen Branter, while Garrachra Glen marks the western extremity. Glen Massan, on the south, completes the enclosure of the area. The hill-side sloping down to Loch Eck side is now a forest area and access to the heights from this side is planned to be up Bernice Glen leading to the Bernice Gap. It is intended that the approach will be from the north end of Loch Eck, turning off the main road at Bridgend, through the Glen Branter estate. It is expected that this route will be open from June to December only.

Another possible access path up to Beinn Mhòr may be from Glen Branter through Glen Shellish. This route would lead you to the watershed separating Glen Shellish from Garrachra Glen, and the ascent from the watershed would be up the northern spur from the summit of Beinn Mhòr.

If it is your wish to use the Bernice or Glen Shellish routes telephone in advance to the Forester (Strachur 29 or 33) to ascertain if it is in order to go that way.

The approach to the hills, if not using either of the access routes, is by way of the Glen Massan road. About a mile out from Sandbank the road turns sharply to the right, along the head of the Holy Loch. At the bend in the road a by-way branches off on the left-hand side and points the way up Glen Massan. It is not far up this road to the entrance gates to Benmore House but, before reaching the gates, go *via* the left-hand turning, which brings you into Glen Massan proper. The road continues up to the head of the glen where the ways divide and the road ceases. You go up the glen as far as Stonefield (check this with your map) and then, leaving the road, you start climbing up the face of the hill-side on your right. This steep slope brings you to a tableland of bog and moss which slopes at a gentler incline up to the top of the hill. This is no craggy mountain, but rather the highest point in a fairly wide waste of moorland. Bog-trotting is perhaps a better description than hill-climbing for to-day.

From the summit of Beinn Mhòr, follow the ridge leading to Bernice Glen, but, at the Bernice Gap, turn west to the head of Glen Shellish. Then go up to the head-waters of the Glen, over the watershed and down the bare and bleak Garrachra Glen to the head of Glen Massan which, in turn, brings you back to the main road at the head of the Holy Loch.

There is a frequent bus service all the year round between

Dunoon and Strone (Ardentinny bus) and a less frequent service between Dunoon and Whistlefield Hostel (Strachur bus).

Fourth day.
THE WHISTLEFIELD–STRONE RANGE

Access : From Gairletter on Loch Long. From Strone. From the head of Puck's Glen. From Glen Finart *via* Drynain Glen. From Inverchapel at the south end of Loch Eck.

Hostels : Strone and Whistlefield.

Bus services : Dunoon-Ardentinny *via* Strone. Dunoon-Strachur *via* Loch Eck side.

Forestry offices : Glen Finart (telephone, Ardentinny 218). Benmore (telephone, Sandbank 201).

This area, roughly the shape of a diamond, has a road along the entire length of its boundary, the southernmost point of which is Strone. From there the eastern boundary is Loch Long as far as Ardentinny, where the Glen Finart road is the dividing line going over the Larach to Loch Eck side at Whistlefield. Going south from here the road follows the line of the loch, then continues through Strath Eachaig to Kilmun and Strone.

There are no roads into or across these hills, but there is a forest road from Gairletter Point on Loch Long side as far as Craigmore Wood—a distance of about three miles. This gives you access to the open range, but it is not possible to say, at this stage, whether this route will be accepted by the Forestry Commission as a recognised access path.

The paths through Puck's Glen in Strath Eachaig lead to within a few yards of the open hill, not very far from Craigmore Wood, and it is possible that the Forestry Commission may make this an access route. If so, there will be an excellent through-route from Gairletter Point on Loch Long side to Puck's Glen and Strath Eachaig.

Another possible access route is from Strone *via* the golf course. An access path through the planted belt and the hillside is reached where there are wide views of the Firth. Once on the hill there are two possible lines to take; Craigmore Wood should be the first objective, and then it is a matter of choice whether you turn to the west for Puck's Glen or to the east for Gairletter.

There is an access route from Glen Finart up Drynain Glen which takes you over the hill and down Inverchapel Glen to the south end of Loch Eck. This route gives the necessary access and approach to Stronchullin Hill, Meall Dubh and Beinn Ruadh.

You have therefore a number of tramping possibilities in this area, but remember that some of the access routes I have given are not yet fixed. Puck's Glen approach, for example, is my own suggestion and at present there is no path out to the hill. The surest approach would appear to be from Gairletter with exit at Inverchapel or *vice versa*.

Fifth day.

BEINN LOCHAIN

Route in brief: Strachur—Strachurmore—River Cur—Socach—Cab Liogan—Beinn Lochain—Curra Lochain—Lettermay Burn—Loch Goil—Lochgoilhead.

Map: Ordnance Survey 1″ scale, No. 65, or special map, " Rothesay and the Firth of Clyde."

Hostel: Whistlefield.

Before dealing with the route given in brief above, reference should be made to the access path at the Coire Ealt. This track starts from the roadside, about three-quarters of a mile from the north end of Loch Eck. Here there is a black-and-white marker, pointing the way up the Coire Ealt through the forest to the hill. Once through the forest you have access to a number of peaks. These are Cnoc na Tricriche (1,986 feet); Sgùrr a' Choinnich (2,148 feet) and Beinn Bheula (2,557 feet). There is a through-route over the hills to the Lettermay Burn and down to Lochgoilhead. By following this route the summit of Beinn Bheula, which marks the boundary at this point of the Forest Park, could be included.

The Forestry Commission map of the southern area shows a June–December track from Ballemeanoch, near Strachur, by way of the Cur Water, but, for to-day's excursion, leave the main road at Strachur, as if going to Ballemeanoch, but turn to the left at Strachurmore up the Socach track. The

Forest Park boundary is the Cur Water as far as the tributary on the right—the Leavanin. (The spelling on the 1876 edition of the Ordnance Survey map is Leamanin.) The Forest Park boundary follows this tributary, and goes on to the summit of Beinn Bheula. Your route is up the Socach track to its end, which is at a bridge over another tributary on the right, called Cab Liogan. Follow this hill stream and, as you ascend, choose your own way to the top of Beinn Lochain which is before you. From the summit descend due south to the mountain pool about 1,300 feet below. Having reached this lochan—marked on the map as Curra Lochain—follow the burn flowing from the eastern end of the water. A strange feature of this mountain pool is that seven streams flow out of it in various directions. The tributary you follow connects with the Lettermay Burn which you then follow down to Lochgoilhead.

The whole of this route, right from Strachur, is outside the National Forest Park although quite near the boundary. It is, however, an all-the-year-round access route to some of the peaks in the Forest Park.

Sixth day.

ARGYLL'S BOWLING GREEN

Route in brief : Lochgoilhead—East side of Loch Goil—Stuckbeg—The Saddle (1,704 feet)—Beinn Reithe (2,141 feet)—Cnoc Coinnich (2,497 feet)—Donich Water—Lochgoilhead.

Map : Ordnance Survey 1″ scale, No. 65, or special map, " Rothesay and the Firth of Clyde."

Hostel : Ardgarten.

Access : Portincaple Ferry and Mark. Stuckbeg and Beach. Coilessan Glen. Donich Water. These routes are open from June to December.

Forestry office : Arrochar (telephone; Arrochar 43).

Argyll's Bowling Green is the name given to the hills between Glen Croe and Loch Goil down the line of Loch Long. There are a number of access paths up to the heights from various points.

To reach The Saddle from Lochgoilhead, follow the track by the loch-side to the derelict house of Stuckbeg and on to

Beach (pronounced Be-ach), also unoccupied. From here there is a track over the hill, between Tom Molach and The Saddle and *via* Corran Lochan, down to the house called Mark (occupied). There is a ferry connection between here and Portincaple and accordingly it is possible to reach Lochgoilhead by train from Glasgow to Whistlefield (Gare Loch), cross by ferry from Portincaple and walk, *via* Beach, to Lochgoilhead. There is not a regular ferry service but the boatman at Portincaple will row a party across on request. There is no ferry service from Mark to Portincaple.

To reach the summit of The Saddle do not descend to Mark from the watershed, but continue up the hill. From the summit it is not a great distance to the north, to reach Beinn Reithe which is about 400 feet higher than The Saddle. From here you should descend to Loch Goil side at Beach, unless you are prepared for a heavy tramp on to Cnoc Coinnich (2,497 feet). If you tackle this further peak, bear in mind that you are faced with the fairly long descent to the Donich Water and Lochgoilhead, or down Coilessan Glen to Loch Long and Ardgarten and do not attempt this unless you are suitably clothed and shod and have the stamina to stay the course; also, do not carry a heavy pack. Keepers and foresters alike all remark on the heavy packs carried by trampers.

There is an access path along the shore of Loch Long from Ardgarten to Mark; but do not attempt it. There was a track at one time but now it is completely overgrown and obliterated for most of the way. It is possible that this route will be opened presently by the Forestry Commission.

Seventh day.
THE DONICH WATER ACCESS PATH

Access : Donich Water path from Lochgoilhead to Glen Croe. Open all the year round.

Map : Ordnance Survey 1″ scale, Nos. 61 and 65.

Hostel : Ardgarten.

Forestry office : Arrochar (telephone, 43).

This access path is an official route from Lochgoilhead to Glen Croe and will, in due course (perhaps by the time you go this way), be marked with indicator posts. From the

Lochgoilhead end the route begins at the main road, just north of the village where the hill stream crosses under the road and where the road for Lettermay branches off to the left. You leave the road on the right by a path to Inveronich. or you can reach it from the road by the village church.

The access path follows the stream—the Donich Water—which, at a higher level, is shown on the map as the Allt Coire Odhair, and crosses the hills before running down to Glen Croe where it joins the main road at " The Little Rest."

If you are approaching this access path from the Glen Croe end, walk for about one and a half miles from Loch Long side to what is called " The Little Rest." On the way you pass the house of the forester on the right-hand side of the road.

At " The Little Rest " follow the burn-side to the junction of the old and the new roads, and then continue by the access path which, as already mentioned, is scheduled to be way-marked.

This track gives access to The Brack and the Coilessan Glen track and also enables you to climb Ben Donich (2,774 feet). The approach to this hill is from Lochgoilhead up the Coire Odhair. Walk for about two miles up the glen from Lochgoilhead, and then strike up the hill on your left. Choose your own route to descend. You can return to Lochgoilhead or to Ardgarten, *via* Coilessan, as you feel inclined.

The Brack is best ascended from Ardgarten and will be dealt with later.

Eighth day.

LOCH GOIL, GLEN FINART AND LOCH ECK

Route in brief : Loch Goil side—Carrick Castle—Knap—Ardentinny—Glen Finart—Whistlefield.

Walking distance : 17 miles.

Map : Ordnance Survey 1″ scale, No. 65, or special map, " Rothesay and the Firth of Clyde."

Hostel : Whistlefield.

Forestry office : Ardentinny (telephone, Ardentinny 218).

The route from Lochgoilhead to Ardentinny by way of Carrick Castle and Knap has been described in the Firth of

Clyde Hinterland Tour (ninth day) and the way from Arden-tinny to Whistlefield has been dealt with on the tenth day of the same tour. Briefly the route is as follows: From Loch-goilhead follow the road on the south (or west) side of the loch to Carrick Castle, and then follow the hill track over to Knap cottage by the shores of Loch Long. It seems there are two paths, but the one to follow is that which keeps near to the shore all the way. It is marked on the Forest Park map as being open all the year round. The first time I went this way the cottage of Knap was occupied by a thriving family and the children went to school each school-day by motor-boat provided by the Education Authority, but now the cottage is empty.

From Knap cottage the track continues to Ardentinny, which was the first home of a group of Newfoundland lumber men when they came to Scotland at the beginning of the war.

At Ardentinny, go by the road to Whistlefield, up Glen Finart, and over the Larach to Loch Eck side. You will see a forestry nursery in the glen, and as you climb to the water-shed you will pass through a young forest where already the trees are strong and sturdy.

On the roadside, along the stretch of road over the water-shed and on the Loch Eck side, you will find, in season, plenty of blaeberries. A few years ago we spent a family holiday in Glen Finart and never before did we pick and eat so many and such big blaeberries.

Ninth day.

THE REST AND BE THANKFUL

Route in brief : Strachur—St. Catherine's—Glen Kinglas—Butterbridge—Loch Restil—Rest and be Thankful—Glen Croe—Arrochar.

Walking distance : Approximately 20 miles.

Maps : Ordnance Survey 1″ scale, Nos. 61 and 65.

Hostel : Glen Loin or Ardgarten.

The mileage is not given exactly, because you may walk all the way from Whistlefield or you may go either to Glen Loin Hostel or to Ardgarten.

Travel by service bus (on the route Dunoon–Strachur)

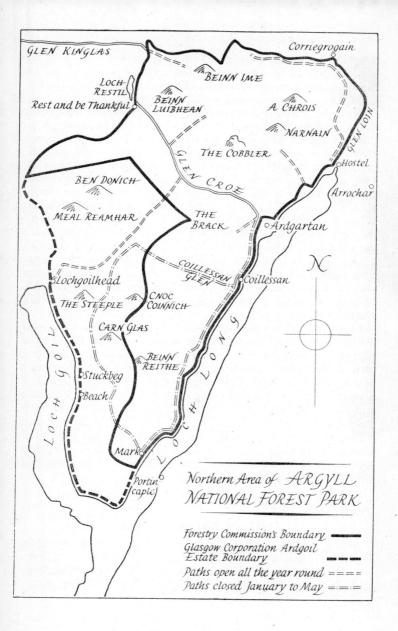

GLEN KINGLAS
Corriegrogain
BEINN IME
LOCH RESTIL
Rest and be Thankful
BEINN LUIBHEAN
A CHROIS
NARNAIN
THE COBBLER
GLEN CROE
Hostel
Arrochar
BEN DONICH
MEAL REAMHAR
THE BRACK
Ardgartan
COILLESSAN GLEN
Coillessan
Lochgoilhead
THE STEEPLE
CNOC COINNICH
CARN GLAS
BEINN REITHE
LOCH GOIL
LOCH LONG
GLEN LOIN
Stuckbeg
Beach
Mark
Portin caple

N

Northern Area of ARGYLL NATIONAL FOREST PARK

Forestry Commission's Boundary ▬▬▬
Glasgow Corporation Ardgoil Estate Boundary ▬ ▬ ▬
Paths open all the year round ═══
Paths closed January to May =·=·=

from the hostel at Whistlefield to Strachur and then walk by the loch-side to St. Catherine's, from which place you follow the route given on the eighth day of the Firth of Clyde Hinterland Tour. This is a road walk all the way.

From St. Catherine's, continue northward until you come to the parting of the ways. One route—to the right—is to Lochgoilhead. You could go that way if you wished, down Hell's Glen and then, a little distance from Lochgoilhead, turn to the left up the road to The Rest and be Thankful. The way recommended—and considered to be the better route—is to go to the left at the parting of the ways above St. Catherine's and join the long road through Glen Kinglas. When you join that glen road, turn to the right and walk to the very end of the glen, at least as far as Butterbridge, where the road leaves the glen and turns right, up the hill through a glen with a long and seemingly unpronounceable name. You pass Loch Restil on the right when traversing this glen and, at the top of the hill, come to The Rest and be Thankful. This is the name given to the point at the top of the hill where the three roads meet.

From the top of the road you look down Glen Croe and see the snake-like road which will bring you right through the glen to the loch-side. If you are going to stay at Ardgarten, turn to the right, a short distance after passing the Forester's house, which is on the left side of the road. If, however, it is your intention to stay at Glen Loin, continue to the loch-side and on to the head of Loch Long. At the head of the loch the road crosses the stream by the Two Shires' Bridge but, before reaching the bridge, you go ahead up the glen by a farm road on your left. You come to the village of Arrochar soon after crossing the Two Shires' Bridge, so you will not have far to go to buy food supplies.

Tenth day.

THE COBBLER GROUP

Access : Main road through Glen Croe to The Rest and be Thankful. Route from Butterbridge for Beinn Ime. Corrie-grogain access route. From Succoth for Narnain. The Sourmilk Burn for The Cobbler. From the top of " The Rest "

Robert M. Adam

ARGYLL NATIONAL FOREST PARK AND THE COBBLER

Robert M. Adam

THE WILDS OF LOCH ECK

ARGYLL NATIONAL FOREST PARK AND LOCH LONG

Robert M. Adam

W. A. Poucher, F.R.P.S.

BEN LOMOND AND LOCH LOMOND

for Beinn Luibhean. From Cobbler Bridge at Laigh Glen Croe to Corrie Croe.

Maps : Ordnance Survey 1″ scale, Nos. 61 and 62.

Hostel : Glen Loin.

Forestry office : Arrochar (telephone, 43).

The area embraced by the title " The Cobbler Group " is bounded by the main road from the Two Shires' Bridge at Arrochar through Glen Croe to The Rest and be Thankful and down to the Butterbridge in Glen Kinglas. Here the march leaves the road, goes east to Beinn Ime and Corrie-grogain, then down Glen Loin back to the Two Shires' Bridge.

Beinn Ime (3,318 feet) is the highest peak in the park (there are 112 higher mountains in Scotland, according to the Munro Tables) and also the farthest north. Access paths to the mountain are numerous. Approach can be made by the Corriegrogain route or from Corrie Croe, but the route from Butterbridge is recommended. If the service bus through to Loch Fyne is operating, make use of it to travel to Butter-bridge at the turning for Kinglas Glen. Just before the bend in the road at the burnt-out Beinn Ime cottage the track leads away to the hill, between the stream and the fence. As you come to the open hill make your own way to the top of Beinn Ime, which is before you, and descend by way of the Corrie Croe route to Glen Croe.

Beinn Luibhean is best approached from the head of " The Rest " with descent to Corrie Croe.

The direct approach to Narnain is by the access route up the face of the hill from the Glen Loin Hostel. This route can also be used for The Cobbler, but the commoner route for this most popular hill is from the Torpedo Station, across the loch from Arrochar.

Follow the right bank of the Sourmilk Burn from the Torpedo Station right up the hill, until you are near the head-waters. Bear away to the left here into the corrie under the summit rocks. Choose your own route to the top, but be careful when negotiating the hole or eye of the rock on the summit.

An alternative to returning the way you came is a descent *via* the Corrie Croe route ; another is a return *via* Succoth.

5

You could include Narnain in your return route. It is not so very far away and if you study your map you will find that this is a very attractive extension.

The Cobbler gave its name to Scotland's first climbing club and in recent years has been popular with various climbing clubs, among them "The Ptarmigan," "Lomond," "Tricouni" and "Creag Dhu." J. B. Nimlin described The Cobbler climbing grounds as "areas of crag where the sole rugosities are knobs of quartz, horizontal wrinkles and ledges of embedded turf."

In 1940 B. H. Humble and D. Beveridge discovered "The Cobbler Cave" at the foot of the Ramshead Ridge, just off the route to the summit.

Eleventh day.

THE BRACK

Access : From Ardgarten Hostel. Coilessan Glen. From Glen Croe.

Map : Ordnance Survey, 1" scale, No. 65.

Hostel : Ardgarten.

Forestry office : Arrochar (telephone, 43).

There is a short access path right from the back door of Ardgarten Hostel on to the open hill-side. The Warden will show you where the path starts.

To reach the Coilessan access path follow the road down the loch-side to Coilessan to the path going up the glen. Quite a few people take the wrong turning here and, as a result, wander on down the loch-side and eventually find themselves in the wrong glen. When you reach the sheepfold on the north side of Coilessan Glen, look out for a dividing of the path a few yards farther on. Take the right-hand turn and then, two hundred yards farther on, turn left for a hundred yards and then turn right. You are now all set for the glen. At the end of the track, at the open hill-side, you have the summit of The Brack as your immediate objective. A good plan is to climb The Brack from the "back door" access path at Ardgarten and descend down the Coilessan path.[1]

---

[1] Spelling is *Coilessan* on the Ordnance Survey map and *Coilleson* on the Argyll National Forest Park map.

The Brack is a favourite with many hostellers and particularly with the Warden, who says, when describing the climb, " The first half-hour leads through fragrant pine forests and then comes a mixture of bracken, bilberry, heather and an occasional rowan tree; then the steeper slopes, where outcrops of rock beckon the more adventurous spirits."

There is a wee lochan at The Brack plateau with cotton-grass growing round the verges. The Ardgarten Warden likens this small mountain pool to " a jewel in the folds of the mountain."

An alternative route from the summit of The Brack is Cruach Fhiorach.

Note.—This tour could not have been described without the co-operation of the Forestry Commission, and this opportunity is taken to thank not only the authorities in Edinburgh but the forest officers, foresters, keepers, forest workers, wardens and also the womenfolk at the forest houses for their kindly hospitality.

IV

THE FIRTH OF CLYDE HINTERLAND

INTRODUCTION

THE tramper, casting his eyes on Scotland with a view to a fortnight's walking tour, normally does not think of the Firth of Clyde as a good tramping area. He is apt to think of Rothesay and Dunoon as reproductions of Blackpool. Such a supposition is quite wrong, as both resorts make wonderful centres for an almost unlimited number of tramping excursions. The area to be covered in this tour embraces the hills around the Gare Loch, Loch Long, Loch Goil, Loch Eck and the Holy Loch, as well as the island of Bute. The uplands and moorlands on the south side of the Firth are also explored and, altogether, you have a very comprehensive tour of the Firth of Clyde Hinterland.

First day.

Travel to Wemyss Bay from Glasgow (Central).

Second day.

THE BACK OF THE WORLD

Route in Brief: Inverkip—Roman Bridge—Sheilhill Glen —Compensation Reservoir—Kelly Cut—Kelly Reservoir— Back of the World—Noddsdale Road—Loch Thom—Sheilhill Glen—Inverkip.

Walking distance: 15 miles.

Map: Ordnance Survey, special map, "Rothesay and the Firth of Clyde."

Follow the by-way that leads off the main road which turns and twists from Inverkip to the Roman Bridge and

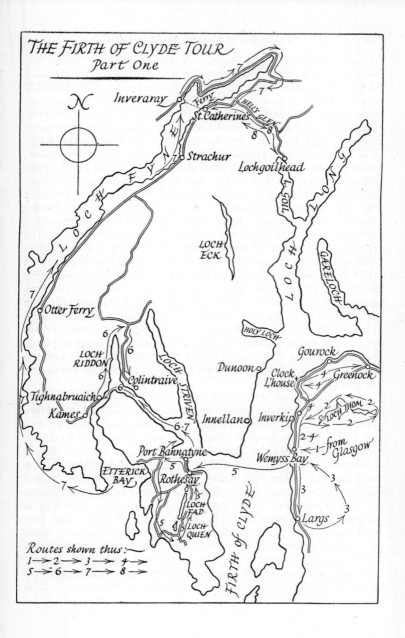

THE FIRTH OF CLYDE TOUR
Part One

N

Inveraray
Ferry
St. Catherines
HELL'S GLEN
Strachur
Lochgoilhead
LOCH FYNE
LOCH GOIL
LOCH ECK
GARELOCH
Otter Ferry
HOLY LOCH
LOCH RIDDON
Colintraive
LOCH STRIVEN
Dunoon
Gourock
Clock L'house
Greenock
Tighnabruaich
Kames
Innellan
Inverkip
LOCH THOM
from Glasgow
Port Bannatyne
Wemyss Bay
ETTERICK BAY
Rothesay
LOCH FAD
LOCH QUIEN
Largs
FIRTH OF CLYDE

Routes shown thus :—
1→ 2→ 3→ 4→
5→ 6→ 7→ 8→

crosses Sheilhill Glen Burn. A short distance from this bridge turn to the right and walk uphill with the long grassy slopes of Dunrod Hill on your left-hand side, with Sheilhill Glen, of which more will be seen on the return journey, on your right. At the head of the road you come to the Compensation Reservoir, but do not follow the road beyond the gate; instead, take the path on the right, which follows the Kelly Cut or Aqueduct across the moor to the Kelly Reservoir. And now begins the best part of the walk. The road uphill from Inverkip to Cornerlees has been a mere introduction, but once you leave it and take to the path, you are treading the wild, open moorlands. Consulting the map, you observe that you are crossing what is called Blood Moss, and looking around you, you will see far-away Kintyre where, in the spring, long wisps of smoke betoken burning heather; you will see the boats passing and re-passing on the highway of the Clyde, majestic liners and deep-laden freight vessels coming from and going to all the corners of the earth and carrying people of all nations. You will pick out Rothesay, the line of the Cowal shore and various vantage points in Bute. The view of Arran, too, will give you delight, and from certain points on the mainland one sees the outline of what is popularly called the Sleeping Warrior—an outline that is created by the conformation of various peaks on the island harnessed to a little imagination.

After an all too short walk across the moorland, you come to the reservoir from which commences the Aqueduct. Here you can rest and lunch. After lunch, continue on your way by following the stream that feeds the reservoir. A march fence also follows the line of this stream and so you should have little difficulty in keeping in the right direction. You will find the going very heavy, but if your feet are to be wet anyhow, just plough through the marsh and enjoy the coolness of the experience. The moorland you are now crossing is marked on the map as " The Back of the World," and you will agree that its loneliness suggests such a name. After you have negotiated the moorland, you come to the road in Noddsdale, where you turn to the left and, after a short distance, turn to the left again along the road that brings you back to Cornerlees and the Compensation Reservoir. It is too tame an affair to follow the road all the way down and so it is suggested that you cut down into the glen itself and follow the stream right away down to the Roman Bridge. From the Roman Bridge you return to Inverkip by the way you came and so to Wemyss Bay.

Third day.

BRISBANE GLEN AND DOUGLAS PARK

Route in brief : Wemyss Bay—Largs—Greeto Falls—Douglas Park—Brisbane Glen—Wemyss Bay.

Walking distance : 10 miles.

Map : Ordnance Survey, special map, " Rothesay and the Firth of Clyde."

Travel by bus from Wemyss Bay to Largs and visit the Douglas Park. At the high vantage point a view is presented similar to, but not so extensive as, that from the Kelly Reservoir. The view is dominated by the outline of Arran and from this point you should have a clear impression of the Sleeping Warrior (or should we say " Lord Brougham lying asleep in his night-cap " ?). Unlike the Isle of Arran, the high land around Largs is not free to the rambler. The Gogo Burn and Glen at Largs is private and it is necessary to obtain permission to enter at the keeper's lodge, where a key is provided for the gate leading to the path through the glen. This path takes you right up to the Greeto Falls, which are well worth a visit.

Continue along the promenade as far as St. Colombo Church. Here you turn up Douglas Street, at the top of which turn to the left for Noddsdale Road, where the Knock Hill is on your left.

The entrance gates to Brisbane House are on your left, too, and a little farther on is the right-of-way into the glen. You will recognise this by-way because across the road in Noddsdale is a letter-box marked " Noddsdale." From here make your way through the glen, where the " Prophet's Grave " marks the burial place of the Rev. William Smith, a martyr to the plague of 1644. It would appear that, when dying, he stated that if two holly trees were planted, one at each end of his grave, the plague would not appear in Largs so long as the trees were kept from meeting. Brisbane House was at one time the residence of General Sir Thomas Makdougall-Brisbane, who died in 1860. He was Governor of New South Wales from 1821–5 and gave his name to the capital.

The glen is all too short, but what there is of it is good. You follow the grassy road to the bend where the road ceases, and the track continues to bear away at right angles on your left. This track is ill-defined, but you should have no difficulty in finding your way to the top of the hill and the glory of the Clyde. If you wish, you may climb the Knock Hill and then descend by the side of the woodland to the Inverkip road which will bring you back to Wemyss Bay. If you can time your visit to this high vantage point to coincide with the sunset you will have a wonderful opportunity of watching the sun setting behind Arran. As the light recedes from the sky it appears to be drawn towards Arran, to sink in long flaming shafts down behind the inky blackness of the sky-line, and as these flaming banners disappear one by one, the darkness gathers until all is a deep purple except for a line of fire along the Arran Hills. Finally, this light, too, goes out. It is night, and you are alone on the hill.

Fourth day.

SEARCHING FOR AN ECHO

Route in brief : Bus to Gourock—Ashton—Trumpet Hill —Primrose Crags—Echoing Rocks—Faulds Farm—Cloch Lighthouse.

Walking distance : 7 miles.

Map : Ordnance survey, special map, " Rothesay and the Firth of Clyde."

Travel on the Gourock bus from Wemyss Bay, alight at Ashton and then follow the by-way leading uphill to the farm at Trumpet Hill, beyond which is a belt of trees. From now on you have the Firth of Clyde and its attendant mountains in full view. On each of your excursions from Wemyss Bay, whenever you climb to a vantage point you have almost the same view, but on each occasion there is something different. From the vantage point on the golf course, where you are now, you see farther east, with the Holy Loch, Gare Loch and the Ben Lomond group of mountains in full view. After following the track through the whin bushes, you come to the second disused quarry and, on the far side of it, you follow the line of dykes which leads you to the hill where one line of dykes joins another at right angles. Here you turn to the right along the fairway, as far as the tee, then left to enjoy the scramble up the Primrose Crags. Incidentally, this is a name given to the rocks by myself; no name appears on the map, but in springtime these rocks are made bright by primroses. Having reached the summit of the hill there is an even wider view of the Firth stretching right away to Ailsa Craig. This, I think, gives you the most extensive view of any of the walks from Wemyss Bay. You will observe that " The Sleeping Warrior," seen from this point, appears to have his knees up. Across the moor there is a dam and a stone dyke and, leading from it, at right angles, another runs in the direction of the Cloch Lighthouse. Follow this dyke and soon you cross the Echoing Dyke on your right and come to the Echo Rocks. Return across the golf course to Faulds Farm. There are other ways downhill, but these are private and so I cannot recommend them. At Faulds Farm you come to the main road and board the bus for Wemyss Bay.

Fifth day.

THE ISLAND OF BUTE, BARONE HILL
AND LOCH FAD

Route in brief : Steamer from Wemyss Bay to Rothesay— Bus to Kames Bay, Port Bannatyne—Through the golf course to Barone Hill—Descend to Loch Fad and Loch Quien— Return to Rothesay.

Walking distance : 12 miles.

Map : Ordnance Survey, special map, " Rothesay and the Firth of Clyde."

Travel by steamer from Wemyss Bay to Rothesay and then by bus to Kames Bay where you begin your walk by climbing up the steps to come to the golf course and Barone Hill, from which there are splendid views of Bute and the Firth. After enjoying the view from Barone Hill, which is the highest point in the Island of Bute, you descend to a farm marked on your map as Eskechraggan. A short distance below the summit you come to a cart-track that brings you to the farm, beyond which you come to the Greenan Loch, the head of which you skirt on your way to Loch Fad. The by-way you are on connects Eskechraggan Farm with the main road from Rothesay to St. Ninians Bay. Follow this road for about one mile and you come to a fork where you turn to the left and, soon afterwards, take to the hill-side to climb Barmore Hill, which has three or four successive summits, from the highest of which you have a very fine view of the island. Between Rothesay and Scalpsie Bay there are three lochs: the first is Kirk Dam, the second Loch Fad and the third the Quien Loch. When viewed from the top of Bishop's Seat above Dunoon, these three lochs appear as one, and also give the impression of being connected with the sea at Rothesay and Scalpsie. From the top of Barone Hill you look down on these three lochs and, beyond, see right across the uplands of Southern Bute as far as Garroch Head. From here the Island of Arran is seen to its fullest advantage and " The Sleeping Warrior " is seen from yet another angle. From the summit of Barone Hill make your way downhill to come between Loch Fad and the Quien Loch, beyond which is the main road leading back to Rothesay Bay. Possibly you may not like the hard road, in which case skirt the field to the loch-side and follow the road down to the wall that separates Loch Fad from the Kirk Dam. Across the waters of Loch Fad you will see Barmore Wood, in which is situated Kean's cottage.

Rothesay has a long history and has known many rulers. In 1400 it was created a Royal Burgh by Royal Charter. This charter brought prosperity to the town, but when Campbeltown was likewise created a Royal Burgh it would appear that a great deal of trade was taken from Rothesay. Matters were apparently evened up in 1765, when Rothesay was made a Custom House Station and, later, a licensed port for herring fishing. Possibly during your stay in Rothesay you may see the Fishery cruiser which patrols the waters of this area. It is always on the outlook for illegal fishing, either in prohibited waters or with illegal types of nets. Occasionally one reads of an exciting chase which culminates in a court case, and if the accused is found guilty, not only is there a heavy fine but his nets may be confiscated.

Sixth day.

THE KYLES OF BUTE

Route in brief : Travel by steamer from Rothesay to Tighnabruaich in the Kyles of Bute—Loch Riddon—Colintraive—Return by steamer to Rothesay.

Walking distance : 15 miles.

Map : Ordnance Survey, special map, " Rothesay and the Firth of Clyde."

Before setting out you should study the time-tables to make sure that you have sufficient time to carry out this excursion. If you miss the last boat from Colintraive the only possibility is to be ferried across to the Island of Bute and face a seven-mile walk to the bus at Kames. This, in all, involves a walk of over twenty miles.

The journey by steamer is all too short but, as you go, you can pick out the road you will walk on the way to Colintraive and you can also see the long shore road that leads from Kames to the ferry opposite Colintraive. Then the boat threads its way through the Burnt Islands and round the Maids of Bute, those queer upstanding rocks at the northern end of the island, to bring you to Tighnabruaich Pier. From the village, follow up the loch-side, round the bay, to come to Rudha Ban. Half-way round the Bay you find a footpath that leads up the hill on the west side of the burn; follow this path, which, after a short distance, crosses the burn and then the slope of the hill to come to the Black Burn. Across this stream the path winds uphill, keeping above the woodland, later to descend to the loch-side. For some distance now it keeps almost to the loch-side and, near the head of the loch, joins the metalled road at Ormidale Lodge. From the head of the loch you have about two miles of walking before coming to a by-way on the right which takes you across the glen. It is not possible to cross the stream before this and for this reason you are faced with a walk down the other side of the glen. You join the road on the east side of Glen Riddon at Auchenbreck, from which point it is about six miles to Colintraive.

Should you find it necessary to cross the ferry at Colintraive and walk home, the going is not unpleasant. It is possible that at the time of your visit the boat may not call at Colintraive. In that case it is suggested that you go by boat to Brodick, on the Isle of Arran, and employ the time ashore by walking to Glen Rosa.

Seventh day.

LOCH FYNE

Route in brief: Steamer from Rothesay to Inveraray—Walk round the head of the loch to St. Catherine's.

Walking distance: 15 miles.

Map: Ordnance Survey, special map, " Rothesay and the Firth of Clyde."

You travel from Rothesay to Inveraray by steamer and, upon arrival at Inveraray, have the alternative of being thoroughly lazy, travelling by ferry across to St. Catherine's and so avoiding a day's walking. If, however, you wish to tramp round the head of the loch—and it is worth it—send your kit across by ferry and set off along the road that follows round the shore of Loch Shira. On the far side of the loch you look across the waters to see the township of Inveraray, made conspicuous by its white arches which give it quite a foreign appearance. After that the road skirts Strone Point and you have a stretch of nearly six miles to the head of Loch Fyne, on the way passing the old castle on Dundarave Point. At the head of the loch the road crosses the River Fyne, which has come down from the jumble of hills you see away up the glen. Having crossed the river, the road follows the line of the hills and the loch and, after about a mile and a half of walking, brings you to Cairndow. Here, a little beyond the church, the road winds through the woodlands away from the loch into Glen Kinglas. This is a long, bare glen that cuts through the hills to the " Rest and be Thankful." Keep to this road for about half a mile and you see a by-way, on your right, leading downhill to cross the stream. This is the way to St. Catherine's, and your route for to-day. This by-way, after crossing the stream and climbing a short distance to the shoulder of the hill, follows the top of the woodlands, which hide the view of the loch. At the end of the woodlands you come to the road leading to Lochgoilhead, while ahead your road winds downhill to St. Catherine's.

If you are not carrying a tent with you, you will find there is little accommodation apart from the hotel, but if you care to walk on a further four miles to Strachur there is a wider choice.

Eighth day.

THROUGH HELL'S GLEN

Route in brief : St. Catherine's—Glen Kinglas road—Hell's Glen—Glen Goil—Lochgoilhead.

Walking distance : 10 miles.

Maps : Ordnance Survey, special maps, " Rothesay and the Firth of Clyde " and " Trossachs."

From St. Catherine's you retrace your footsteps of the previous day until you come to the turning on the right to Hell's Glen. By following the road from Hell's Glen to Lochgoilhead you have a total walking distance for the day of ten miles. If, however, you wish to be more strenuous you should continue along the road of the previous day to Glen Kinglas and follow right up it to the heart of the hills. As you follow this road you wonder how you are going to get out of the glen. You appear to come to a dead-end, but eventually you find that the road branches sharply to the right, crossing the stream and climbs uphill to Loch Restil and thence to the " Rest and be Thankful." Here, at the top of a hill, you look back in one direction on the way you have come, in another down Glen Croe and in a third down Gleann Mor. The road down Gleann Mor, which is a little more than a grassy track, brings you to the entrance of Hell's Glen where you join the direct route from St. Catherine's.

At the top of the road above St. Catherine's, if you do not intend to do the extension, you turn to the right, to climb up the zigzag road into Hell's Glen. From your map you will observe that you can cut off quite a considerable corner by following a grassy track that joins the road a little more than a mile from the cross-roads. The mouth of the glen is well wooded where the road winds downhill and joins the road coming down Gleann Mor. At the junction of these roads you have the alternative of following the main road, or of keeping to the grassy track that follows the other side of the river. You must join this track where the main road through Hell's Glen crosses the stream on the Hell's Glen side of the bridge.

On the previous day's excursion it was suggested that you might find accommodation in Strachur, which is four miles down the road from St. Catherine's. If you have done so, it will not be necessary to tramp back to St. Catherine's and so through Hell's Glen. Instead you have an opportunity of a wild walk through the hills from Strachur to Lochgoilhead. There is a track, leading along the northern side of the River Cur, which brings you to the meeting of the waters beyond Socach cottage. At the waters' meeting you follow the main right-hand stream which is marked on your map as Cab Liogan. Follow this stream right up to the head-waters and so to the summit of Beinn Lochain whence you look down on to Loch Goil and so can pick your own way downhill. Two streams rise near the summits of the mountains; one of these can be followed to the point where it joins the Lettermay Burn which, in turn, shows the way to the house of Lettermay and the main road. A mile of walking brings you to Lochgoilhead. This alternative is dealt with in the Argyll National Forest Park chapter (Fifth day).

Ninth day.
LOCH GOIL AND ARDENTINNY

Route in brief : Road alongside Loch Goil—Carrick Castle—Hill path to Knap cottage and Ardentinny—Bus from Ardentinny to Strone.

Walking distance : 11 miles.

Map : Ordnance Survey, special map, " Rothesay and the Firth of Clyde."

From Lochgoilhead the road follows along the side of Loch Goil all the way to Carrick Castle. Soon after leaving Lochgoilhead you pass the opening to Lettermay Glen to come in time to Douglas Pier. From this point the road winds through the woodlands, sometimes on the side of the loch and some-

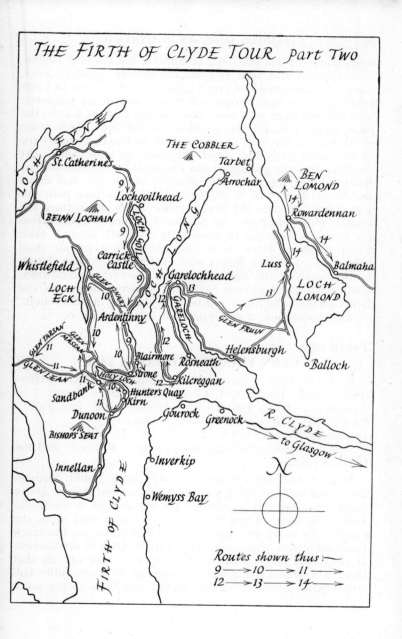

THE FIRTH OF CLYDE TOUR part Two

LOCH FYNE

St. Catherine's

THE COBBLER

Tarbet
Arrochar

BEN LOMOND
14

Lochgoilhead
9

Rowardennan
14

BEINN LOCHAIN

LOCH GOIL

LOCH LONG

14

Luss

Carrick Castle

Whistlefield

GLEN FINART

Garelochhead
13

LOCH LOMOND
13

Balmaha

LOCH ECK

10

12

GARELOCH

Ardentinny

9

GLEN FRUIN

GLEN TARSAN

GLEN MASSAN

10

10

Blairmore

Rosneath

Helensburgh

11

GLEN LEAN

11

HOLY LOCH

11 10

Strone

12

Kilcreggan

Balloch

Sandbank

11

Hunters Quay

Kirn

Gourock

Greenock

R. CLYDE
to Glasgow

Dunoon

BISHOP'S SEAT

Innellan

Inverkip

N

Wemyss Bay

FIRTH OF CLYDE

Routes shown thus:—
9 → 10 → 11 →
12 → 13 → 14 →

times partly up the hill. All around are the knobbly heights of Argyllshire and, near at hand, the shining waters of Loch Goil. As you come to Carrick Castle you see across to Loch Long but your view of this loch is not particularly extensive. You will see from your map that, beyond Carrick Castle, the path wanders round the shoulder of the hill. This route is shown on the map of the Argyll National Forest Park as an access path and could, therefore, be your route. At one time the way recommended and used by the shepherd at Knap cottage was over the shoulder of the hill and down the Knap Burn. It is also considered an access path but you should keep to the lower route. From the cottage the track is elusive in parts; at Shepherd's Point it winds across the Clunie woodlands to descend to the back door of Glen Finart House. Here, what appears to be a private road brings you to Glen Finart and Ardentinny. Glen Finart houses some of the nurseries of the Forestry Commission; whole fields of young trees have been planted in neat rows, and labels indicate the name and time of planting of each batch.

Accommodation at Ardentinny or at nearby Blairmore.

Tenth day.

GLEN FINART AND LOCH ECK

Route in brief: Route 1.—Ardentinny Church—Stronchullin Hill—Inverchapel Glen—Loch Eck. Route 2.—Ardentinny—Glen Finart—Whistlefield—Loch Eck side—Puck's Glen—Holy Loch—Hunter's Quay.

Walking distances: 1.—12 miles. 2.—16 miles.

Map: Ordnance Survey, special map, " Rothesay and the Firth of Clyde."

Near Ardentinny Church a by-way leads uphill, through the woodlands, to bring you to the moorland stream above them. Follow this stream to the summit of Stronchullin Hill (1,798 feet). From the summit you must walk along the ridge to the north and then bear downhill to the west to reach the head-waters of Inverchapel Glen (the Glen of the Stones). If you study the 1″ Ordnance Survey map you will see that there is a stream rising near the summit of Stronchullin Hill which flows down the western slope, then turns to the south

SANDBANK AND HOLY LOCH

Valentine, Dundee

Robert M. Adam

THE EAST LOMOND HILLS

down the corrie between Meall Dubh and Stronchullin Hill.
Should you mistakenly follow this stream you will find yourself, in the course of time, back again at Loch Long side.
On the northern side of the ridge leading up to Meall Dubh
is the source of the Inverchapel Burn, the stream which you
should follow. It is particularly rough going down this glen.
Where the main road crosses the stream turn to the right,
to Loch Eck side. A less strenuous alternative is to take the
Glen Finart road from Ardentinny, by Glen Finart House,
right up the Glen to Loch Eck side. You have five miles of
walking here through a wide and pleasant valley with hills
rising on either side to the 2,000-feet level. After about two
miles of walking you pass Drynain Glen on your left—a
glen which invites you to its loneliness. At the head of the
road you drop down to Whistlefield Inn and join the main
road that follows the eastern shore of Loch Eck. At Whistlefield Inn there is a milestone telling you that it is twelve miles
to Dunoon. This means that you have eleven miles of walking
to Hunter's Quay, which is your destination for to-day. The
road hugs the waterside all the way, following a succession of
bends, to come to the Cothouse Inn beyond which you have
little more than a mile of walking to bring you to the end of
the loch. The road now passes the wide mouth of Inverchapel
Glen, after which you come to the entrance to the Benmore
estate. The entrance gates are sometimes referred to as
" The Golden Gates," but the real " Golden Gates " are at
the Glen Massan entrance. It should be understood that
these gates are not made of gold, but at one time the iron-
work was covered with gilt. A very short distance after
passing Uig Farm, on the right, you reach a bridge which
carries you, and the road, across one of the many hill streams.
Immediately on this side of the bridge is the entrance to the
famous Puck's Glen, planned by the Forestry Commission.
You follow the path which winds round dark, mysterious
pools and climbs up craggy bits alongside leaping waterfalls
to come to the summer-house near the top of the hill. The
roof of this summer-house is crowned with a statuette of
Puck. In front of the house, seats command a view, through
a lane of trees, of the heights surrounding Loch Eck. From
the summer-house another track leads down to the main

6

entrance. Here turn to the left and follow the main road back to Hunter's Quay.

Eleventh day.

THE THREE GLENS—GLEN MASSAN, GLEN TARSAN, GLEN LEAN

Route in brief : Hunter's Quay—Bus to Glen Massan road-end—Glen Massan—Glen Tarsan—Glen Lean—Dalin-longart—Sandbank—Hunter's Quay.

Walking distance : 15 miles. From Glen Massan road-end back to Sandbank bus terminus.

Map : Ordnance Survey, special map, " Rothesay and the Firth of Clyde."

Travel by bus from Hunter's Quay to Glen Massan road-end. You will require to travel on the Dunoon–Ardentinny bus service for this journey, or on the Sandbank bus, and walk the other mile and a half to the Glen Massan road-end. Here you start the real walking of the day and for the first mile and a half keep to the foot of the hills where you see the nurseries of the State Forest. Before long you come to the bridge that crosses the River Massan, beyond which your road bears to the left, keeping by the side of the stream. A little beyond the " Golden Gates " you see Corasik Glen opening out, the slopes of which have been planted with trees to a considerable height.

Farther up the glen you pass a picturesquely situated cottage before coming to the Falls of Glen Massan, where the leaping waters have carved the rocks into smooth pot-holes. After passing the falls you have a long, bare road that leads to the heart of the hills and, presently, reaches Glen Massan Farm, where you follow the road a short distance towards Garrachra, then left across the river at the gate and follow the path leading into Glen Tarsan. The track is not particularly well defined, but there is no mistaking the fact that you are in the glen and that you must work up to the watershed. At the watershed you look down the boggy, bare and bleak Glen Tarsan and, in course of time, you come to the road in Glen Lean where you have a glimpse of Loch Striven, a sea loch, the long arm of which stretches up from

Strone Point. Do not confuse this Strone Point, at the entrance to the Kyles of Bute, with the Strone Point at the head of Loch Long. Having reached the road in Glen Lean you have a further six miles of walking to bring you back to the bus at Sandbank. On the way you come to the village of Clachaig and so to the road at Dalinlongart.

Twelfth day.

ROSNEATH PENINSULA AND GARELOCHHEAD

Route in brief : Hunter's Quay—Steamer to Kilcreggan—Loch Long side and over the hill to the Gare Loch—Main road to Garelochhead.

Walking distance : 9 miles.

Map : Ordnance Survey, special map, " Rothesay and the Firth of Clyde."

On this day you say good-bye to the Cowal shore and travel by steamer from Dunoon or Kirn to Kilcreggan. At Kilcreggan Church you follow the high road that leads round the Rosneath Peninsula to Loch Long side. You will see from your map that one road hugs the shore to Coulport while a secondary road follows a line higher up the hill. It is more interesting to follow this high road; there is no traffic and you have a more extensive view of the Firth of Clyde and its attendant mountains. There is a track across the hills, as you will see from your map, but it is ill-defined. If, however, you choose to follow this route, there is no danger of being lost. The hill rises to no great height and no matter in which direction you walked it would not be long before you came back to civilisation. It is, however, very boggy in parts and so you should be prepared for wet feet. The track over the hill from Cove to Rosneath leads on to the moorlands from Cursnoch Farm, but the route advised for to-day is along the high road past Knockderry Farm. Beyond it, two more miles of walking bring you to the road that winds over the hill to Meikle Rahaen on the Gare Loch. At Meikle Rahaen turn to the left up the Gare Loch side and you come to Garelochhead at the head of this sea-loch. In the evening follow the road uphill to Whistlefield Station and then follow the track down to Portincaple

Ferry. Here you are on Loch Long side, looking across the headland that divides Loch Long from Loch Goil. A small island juts out from the headland and has a Gaelic name which is quite unpronounceable but which, in English, is said to mean " The Isle of the Dogs." As the sun goes down you make your way back again to Garelochhead and so to bed after another glorious day of tramping.

Thirteenth day.
OVER THE HILLS TO LOCH LOMOND

Route in brief: Garelochhead—Faslane Bay—Glen Fruin —Auchingaich—Auchingaich Burn—Beinn Tharsuinn—Glen Finlas—Loch Lomond side to Luss.

Walking distance : 12 miles.

Map : Ordnance Survey, special map, " Loch Lomond and the Trossachs."

Leave Gare Loch side by the road that leads from Faslane Bay (The Bay of Broken Ships) to Glen Fruin (The Glen of Weeping). The name is said to be derived from the fact that the Colquhouns and the Macgregors fought in this glen in 1603. Whether or not the derivation is correct, it would appear from the accounts handed down that the battle was a terrible conflict in which no quarter was given. The story of this wild battle is given in Sir Walter Scott's *Rob Roy.*

Having descended into Glen Fruin and reached the Auchingaich Farm, you leave the road and follow the Auchingaich Burn up to the head-waters. There are no tributaries joining this stream until some distance up the glen, but you should remember to follow the first tributary on the right, which winds a tortuous course through queer formations of the hill. Near the head-waters this tributary becomes three, but it matters little which you follow.

The first visit I paid to this glen was on the occasion of a club excursion which I was leading. I had not been this way before and when we came to the head-waters of the stream we were enveloped in a heavy hill mist. I knew that I should continue to go uphill, and that at the summit I should descend steeply down the crags of Beinn Tharsuinn. In this way, according to the map, I should descend into Glen

Finlas. We set off in the silent mist and in due course came to a summit where, although we could not see, we could feel that we were on the edge of a steep drop. We knew this because of the cold wind rushing up the glen. We descended the steep slope in a manner wonderful to behold: not always quite safe and not always quite elegant. However, we came below the mist without accident and at once took out our maps to check our position. We were bewildered, however, by the fact that in the glen immediately below us was a grey-looking loch. The map did not show any sheet of water in Glen Finlas or in Glen Luss, so where could we be? The map offered no solution, so we trudged downhill and then alongside the loch, the head of which was dammed up as a reservoir. In the lower part of the glen we followed a metalled road and, eventually, came out on Loch Lomond side. At the first milestone we were able to make a definite check with the map and it was then that we discovered that we had come down Glen Finlas after all. There was still the mystery of this reservoir, however, and we realised that we had discovered an omission on the Ordnance Survey map. Whether or not this is a mistake I cannot say, because the map I was using was revised up to 1904. (It is shown on the 1924 revision.)

Having negotiated the Luss Fells and reached Loch Lomond side there is little more of walking ere Luss is reached.

Fourteenth day.
BEN LOMOND AND LOCH LOMOND SIDE

Route in brief : Cross the loch from Luss to Rowardennan —Climb Ben Lomond and return to Glasgow by boat and train from Rowardennan.

Walking distance : One mountain.

Alternative excursion : Cross the loch from Luss to Rowardennan—Walk to Balmaha and climb the Conic Hill—Return by boat from Balmaha.

Walking distance : 4 miles and one hill.

Map : Ordnance Survey, special map, " Loch Lomond and the Trossachs."

The directions for the climb are simple. After you have disembarked from the boat at Rowardennan Pier, turn to the right along the road to come to Rowardennan Hotel. Here you see the commencement of the path for the summit. The track is well defined all the way. The first stage of the journey is from Rowardennan to the Resting Stone and is across the marshy lowlands, while the next stage is by the steep shoulder of the long ridge at the top of which you come to the Half-way Well at the 1,500-feet mark. At the end of the ridge you see the pimple which marks the summit of Ben Lomond. The path now zigzags steeply uphill and, after skirting the northern corrie, brings you to the summit at 3,192 feet.

The normal time for ascent and descent is approximately three and a half hours. This mountain is perhaps the most widely known in all the world and certainly much better known than the other Ben Lomonds of which there are three; one in Australia, another in Utah and yet another in New Zealand.

At the end of 1928 a correspondent of one of the Glasgow newspapers suggested that the summit of Ben Lomond might be crowned with a mountain-view indicator. The suggestion was taken up and the result was that, on the Spring Holiday of 1929, some 2,600 people climbed Ben Lomond to witness the opening ceremony. The work of building the indicator and preparing the chart was undertaken by voluntary helpers. Each Sunday, throughout the winter, parties climbed the Ben, carrying with them the necessary equipment—iron bars for the framework of the cairn, a heavy steel plate and a sheet of glass for the indicator table, hammers, heavy chisels and cement—all were man-handled to the top. As a result of the interest shown by the general public in this event an opportunity was taken to band together the Rambling Clubs in the West of Scotland. The upshot was that the Glasgow and West of Scotland Ramblers' Federation was formed. Out of this grew the Scottish Ramblers' Federation and the Rucksack Club of Scotland, which was responsible for the erection of the first youth hostel in Great Britain.

V

THE FORTH AND THE CLYDE

INTRODUCTION

MANY people, when contemplating a walking tour in Scotland, forget that the central part between Edinburgh and Glasgow contains a very fine tramping district. It contains the favourite places of the Edinburgh and Glasgow rambler. Every type of scenery you could wish for will be found on this tour. You will be introduced to the Pentland Hills, the Fifeshire Hills and also the Ochil Hills, which stand, like a watch-dog, between the Highlands and the Lowlands. You will traverse the Campsie Fells and the Strathblane Hills and finish up by visiting Loch Lomond side and the Clyde, to return through Renfrewshire to Glasgow.

First day.

Travel to Edinburgh.

Second day.

PENTLAND HILLS

Route in brief : Colinton tram terminus—The Loan—Howden Glen—Glencorse—Loganlee Reservoir—Scald Law—Kirk Road—Penicuik.

Walking distance : 10 miles.

Map : Ordnance Survey 1″ scale, No. 74.

For to-day's route travel by tram from Princes Street to the Colinton terminus and continue along Woodhall Road for a short distance to come to Dreghorn Loan on the left. You leave the main road and follow the by-way towards the Pentlands. This lane starts as a very correct type of suburban road, but it soon tires of convention and, after a short distance, becomes a shady lane and then a footpath. Looking back across Edinburgh you see the Castle and Arthur's Seat dominating the city. A background is formed by the widening Firth showing Berwick Law and the Bass Rock, while across in Fife, the Lomond Hills stand out like twin humps on the plain. After enjoying this view, head up Howden Glen and follow the path alongside the stream, to climb up to the watershed where you look down to Glencorse. The road you have followed skirts Allermuir Hill and then follows the line between Castlelaw Hill and Woodhouselee Hill. From the top of the watershed you look down into the valley where Glencorse Reservoir is cradled among the steep hills clothed in woodlands. Descend to the loch and join the road that follows the shore right up to where the Logan Burn connects this reservoir with the higher one of Loganlee. R. L. Stevenson, when writing of Glencorse to Mr. Crockett, says: " The dearest burn to me in the world is that which drums and pours, in cunning wimples, in that glen of yours behind Glen Corse Old Kirk."

At the head of Loganlee Reservoir there are two routes open to the rambler. To-day the route is not by Bavelaw but, instead, turn to the left and follow the track steeply uphill and, as you ascend, bear away from the track to your right to come to the summit of Scald Law. Here you have an even more extensive view than from the hill above Colinton, a view that not only takes in Edinburgh but also much of the Pentlands. You will see many peaks, particularly in the south-west, while in the north-west you will see the Ochil Hills with peaks farther north peeping up here and there. Return to the road you left, " The Kirk Road," which brings you down to the main road connecting Carlops with Glencorse and Edinburgh, and at the main road, turn to the left and, after a little more than half a mile, to the right to follow a by-way that later becomes a footpath and brings you into Penicuik—the end of your day's excursion.

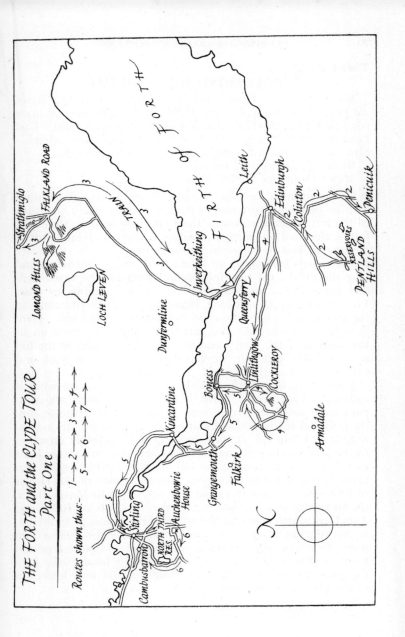

THE FORTH and the CLYDE TOUR
Part One

Routes shown thus:-
1 → 2 → 3 → 4 →
5 → 6 → 7 →

LOMOND HILLS

FALKLAND ROAD

Strathmiglo

LOCH LEVEN

TRAIN

FIRTH of FORTH

Dunfermline

Inverkeithing

Leith

Kincardine

Bo'ness

Queensferry

Edinburgh

Colinton

RESERVOIRS

PENTLAND HILLS

Penicuik

Grangemouth

Falkirk

Linlithgow

COCKLEROY

Armadale

Cambusbarron

Stirling

NORTH THIRD RES.

Auchenbowie House

Third day.

THE LOMOND HILLS OF FIFE

Route in brief : Train from Edinburgh to Falkland Road
via Forth Bridge—Walk from Falkland Road Station by main
road to Falkland—Hill road across the Lomond Hills—East
Lomond Hill—Maspie Den—Arraty Craigs—Drumdreel—
Strathmiglo—Return from Strathmiglo to Edinburgh.

Walking distance : 12 miles.

Map : Ordnance Survey 1″ scale, No. 65.

Go by train to Falkland Road. When leaving the station
turn to the right, to come to the main road where you turn
to the left to walk as far as the four cross-roads. Here you
follow the road to the right, leading towards Falkland Road ;
ignore the first and second turnings on your left (these are
private roads leading up to farmhouses on the hill-sides) and
take the third road that follows up alongside the woodlands
and leads to the moorlands of the Lomond Hills of Fife.
For a while you have a long, straight road, until you come to
the woodlands where the road bears away to the left. Here
you carry on, through the gate, and follow the path up to
the summit of the East Lomond Hill. The height of the hill
is only 1,471 feet but, nevertheless, you have a wide and
extensive view of the country.

Looking to the south, and slightly west, you have what is
called the Five Lochs' View. Four of these lochs are comparatively small reservoirs seen in the middle distance, but
the fifth and the largest is Loch Leven, situated on this side of
Kinross. From the summit descend in a northerly direction
to the road skirting the woodlands when you turn to the right
downhill. At the foot of the hill you see a private road that
turns to the left and takes you into the estate of the House
of Falkland ; follow this road and you come to Maspie Den,
the stream of which crosses under the road you are following.
This Den, which is within the estate of the House of Falkland,
is private, but is open to members of the public on certain
days of each month, though it is necessary to obtain a permit
from the Estate Office of Falkland. At the head of the Den
the path carries you behind the waterfall and thus leads out
of the Den on to the open hill-side.

If you have obtained a permit to walk up Maspie Den you come out on the hill-side near a building which looks very much like a Greek temple; in point of fact it is a disused observatory built by a one-time owner of the House of Falkland who had the building erected for the purpose of studying the stars. Near at hand, across the hill, you see a large stone monument, erected by the tenants of the estate in memory of the astronomer. From this monument you have a wide and extensive view of all the plain surrounding Falkland village.

Descend the hill immediately below the monument and you come to a track leading through the woodlands below the Arraty Craigs to join the path from Balharvie Moss. You are now on the track down to Strathmiglo where the day's walk ends.

Fourth day.

COCKLEROY

Route in brief : Linlithgow—Preston House—Cockleroy—Loch Cote—Armadale Road towards Linlithgow to the Union Canal—Canal bank to Causewayend—Linlithgow Bridge—Linlithgow.

Walking distance : 11 miles.

Map : Ordnance Survey 1″ scale, No. 73.

Follow the road uphill, to the south, from the station. After a very short distance you cross the Union Canal and continue straight up the hill by Rockville House, passing the Friars' Brae on your right. The next turning, on your right, is a quiet by-way along which you walk to Preston House. Here you turn to the left and continue uphill. Looking back you have a view across the town and over the Firth of Forth to the Ochil Hills.

About half a mile farther up the hill from Preston House the road makes a V-shaped bend, but the footpath forms the base and so cuts off the corner. You ignore the next two turnings on your left and come to the woodlands skirting the right-hand side of the road. Where this woodland ceases you leave the road and take to the hill-side that follows the line of the woodlands and soon you see the summit of Cockleroy. It is not a stiff climb, for the hill is only about 800 feet high, but from the top there is an excellent view, uninterrupted on all sides. You see away down the Firth and across to the Lomond Hills of Fife and the Saline Hills, while a little to the west of the Ochil Hills is Stirling, beyond which haze obscures the far-away Perthshire heights. To the east you see the Pentland Hills. To the south you see, immediately below, the pleasant waters of Loch Cote, which is now a reservoir for the town of Bo'ness and you can look across to Airdrie and industrial Lanarkshire.

At the summit of Cockleroy is a small grassy depression known as Wallace's Cradle which is supposed to mark the place where Wallace was accustomed to rest. The western end of the hill is marked by steep crags known as the Fairies' Leap.

Descend by the way you came, but do not follow down to the woodlands; instead, turn to the right, and pass through the gate in the wall and follow the track down to Loch Cote. You have the loch on your left and Lochcote House on the right. The path you follow will bring you to what appears to be a private drive to the house. This path, however, is a right-of-way, as a notice at the other end will inform you. The carriage drive skirts the foot of the Cow Hill, but you should remember that the right-of-way does not continue for the full extent of the drive, and you should follow to the left to Easter Woodside Cottage, where you turn to the right to Wester Woodside Farm and so to the main Armadale road.

At the point where the Loch Cote right-of-way joins the Armadale road you turn to the right, to proceed towards Linlithgow, but you leave the road at the Union Canal and walk along the towing path of the Canal as far as Causeway-end, which is a little way beyond the aqueduct. The feature of the walk along the canal is the aqueduct itself, which carries the canal over the Avon Water. Immediately below the aqueduct the canal enters a leafy region which ends at Causewayend. The route of this canal, which stretches from Port Hopetoun, Edinburgh, to Port Downie on the Forth and Clyde Canal at Falkirk, was recommended by the famous engineer Telford. It was begun in 1818 and completed in four years. At Causewayend leave the watercourse and follow the road down to Linlithgow Bridge, which is on the main

Falkirk–Linlithgow road. Here you turn to the right, when a little more than a mile of walking will bring you back to Linlithgow where you stay overnight.

Fifth day.

GLOUR-O'ER-'EM

Route in brief : Linlithgow—East Port—Bonnytoun Farm —Glour-o'er-'em (Irongath Hills)—Footpath to Kinglass— By-way to Bo'ness—Bus to Grangemouth—Walk to Earl's Gates—Haughs of Airth—Kincardine Road Bridge—Bus to Stirling.

Walking distance : 12 miles.

Maps : Ordnance Survey 1" scale, Nos. 66 and 67.

Leave Linlithgow by the Low Port, which brings you along the eastern shore of Linlithgow Loch. At the head of the Loch turn to the left and follow the road leading to Bonnytoun Farm. A short distance beyond this farm a by-way branches to the left, but ignore this and, farther on, where your road bends round to the right, you will see a footpath leading uphill. It carries you up the slopes of the Irongath Hills (" Glour-o'er-'em ") and brings you to a road near the top of the hill, when you turn to the left to reach the brow. The actual summit of the hill is part of the golf course, and I cannot say whether you have the right to visit the summit. This hill is supposed to be the site of a battle of long ago and relics which have been dug up support this surmise. From this vantage point you have almost as extensive a view as from the summit of Cockleroy. Retrace your steps to the point where the footpath joins the road and here you see the footpath continuing across the road and downhill across the golf course. This is your way to another road which will bring you to Bo'ness, whence you travel by bus to Grange-mouth. From Grangemouth follow the main road towards Falkirk as far as the " Earl's Gates," where you turn to the right along the road towards Skinflats.

After a short distance the road you follow from the " Earl's Gates " brings you to the River Carron, where you turn to the right down to the shores of the Forth and come to a house marked on the map as Heuck. Here you turn to the left and keep on following the by-ways to the Haughs of Airth where you turn to the right, to the Kincardine Road Bridge.

There is an alternative to the walk from " Earl's Gates " to the Kincardine Road Bridge which is worth considering. Instead of walking from the " Earl's Gates," travel by bus along the road to Dunmore. The village of Dunmore sits back from the road and is a little kingdom unto itself. You alight from the bus on the main road at the front door of the village. A little by-way leads you to the village green on three sides of which stand the quaint houses of Dunmore; the fourth side of the green is the river, where Dunmore has its own little harbour, now badly silted up but at one time a harbour to which came a fair amount of trade. After visiting Dunmore you return by bus, through the village of Airth, to the road-end to Kincardine Road Bridge. After you have crossed the Forth you come into the township of Kincardine whence you travel by bus into Stirling. The road to be followed takes you through Alloa and Tullibody, to the north of the Links of Forth, and finally brings you to the main road at Causewayhead, under the shadow of the Wallace Monument. Here the bus turns to the left along the main road to Stirling.

Sixth day.

NORTH THIRD RESERVOIR AND AUCHENBOWIE BY-WAYS

Route in brief : Stirling—St. Ninians—Field of Bannock-burn—North Third Reservoir—Auchenbowie—Bannockburn—St. Ninians—Stirling.

Walking distance : 15 miles.

Map : Ordnance Survey 1″ scale, No. 67.

From Stirling travel by the Glasgow or Edinburgh bus to St. Ninians. At the point where the road forks you see where the main road has skirted the village of St. Ninians.

Follow a short distance along the Denny road and turn to the left up the Borestone Brae to the flag-pole marking the site of the battle of Bannockburn. Beyond the flag-pole the road leads downhill. At the foot of the brae turn to the right to where the road crosses the Bannock Burn. Across the stream the road twists and turns and then makes up its mind to follow the line of the stream and hugs the right-hand bank. Eventually you join the road known as the King's Yetts Road that connects St. Ninian's with Fintry. Turn to the left along this road and, for some distance, you will enjoy the quietness of the woodlands sheltering the Bannock Burn. After leaving the woodlands you come to North Third Farm, beyond which you will follow the by-way that bears off to the left. At the top of the hill you look across to the Sauchie Craigs while, in between, is the North Third Reservoir. These craigs are divided into two groups—the far-away group marking the edge of Middle Third Wood, and the nearer line of craigs the edge of the woodlands of Lewis. In between is the Windy Yetts Glen, on the face of which is an upstanding rock which, when viewed from a particular angle, gives a very clear impression of an old man's bearded face. The reservoir, with its wooded islets, completes the picture.

The road now skirts the loch and brings you down through the estate of Auchenbowie, which houses the Howieburn Fishery. Leaving the fishery, follow the road that leads to the main road at Bannockburn, and from there travel by bus to Stirling.

If you wish to extend your walk, you can do so at the point where the road from North Third Reservoir joins another road into the woodlands some two miles beyond the reservoir. Here you would turn to the left and follow the road leading up to Loch Coulter and Carron Bridge at the four cross-roads. The road continuing south is the Takmadoon Road and leads to Kilsyth; the road to the left goes by Kirk o' Muir to Carron Dam and Fintry, while the road to the east is to Denny. Towards the end of August every year an open-air service is held at Kirk o' Muir to commemorate the Conventicle which was held there in the days of long ago. At Carron Bridge you turn eastwards but, instead of following the road all the way back to Denny, you follow the footpath on the left, or northern, side of the River Carron. This path leads down Carron Glen to South Herbertshire and Denny. Travel by bus to Stirling.

Seventh day.

REST DAY

If you wish for an easy excursion, travel by bus to Tilli-coultry and explore the glen, or go to Alva by bus and visit Alva Glen.   Farther along the Hillfoots Road is Dollar, with its Burn of Sorrow.   Callander is conveniently reached by bus, from which point you can visit the Trossachs.   Also you have an opportunity of visiting the Castle and the Wallace Monument.

Eighth day.

THE KING'S YETTS ROAD

Route in brief: Stirling—Cambusbarron—Gillies Hill—North Third Farm—King's Yetts Road to Randieford Bridge —Loup of Fintry—Fintry.

Walking distance : 15 miles.

Maps: Ordnance Survey 1″ scale, No. 67, and " Loch Lomond " map.

Starting the walk at Murray Place in Stirling, turn along Port Street, then to the right along Park Avenue to the entrance of King's Park and on to Cambusbarron.

At the cross-roads, face to the west and continue for a few yards and turn to the left down what seems a blind alley. At the side of the last house on the right is the path to the Gillies Hill Woodlands.   After a short distance this track is joined by another which comes from Johnny's Bridge at Touch.   These two routes join, and anyone asked to give an opinion upon them would say the two together make a third-class road but a first-class footpath.   Follow it through the woodlands, where it winds at the foot of the Gillies Hill, to come to the King's Yetts Road along the Bannock Burn. At the main road turn to the right, away from Stirling, and carry on to the North Third Farm.   This part of the road has been traversed on a previous excursion, but at North Third Farm you break new ground, for a little beyond the farm the road you previously followed bears to the left, but you continue straight ahead, steadily climbing to come to the King's Yetts Gate, thence across the moors to the Fintry

Robert M. Adam

SIR JOHN DE GRAHAME'S CASTLE, FINTRY HILLS

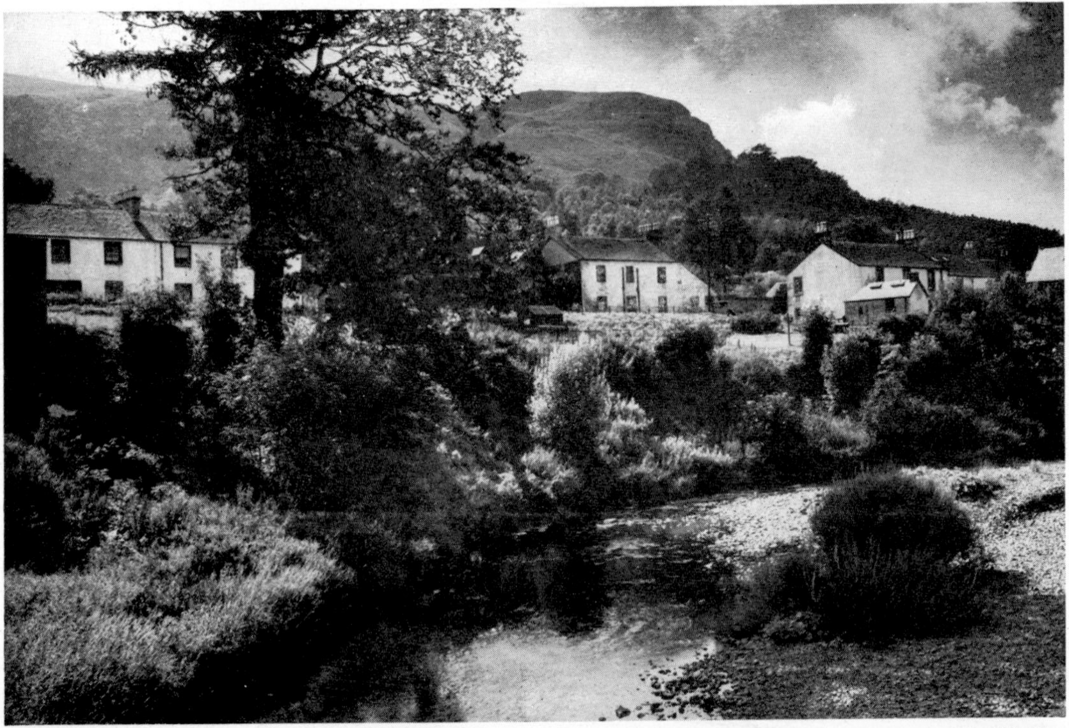

Robert M. Adam

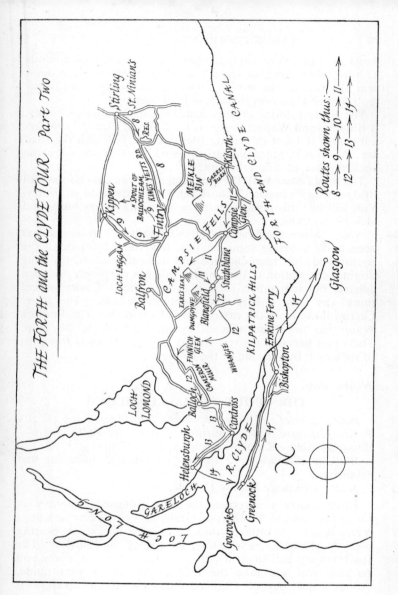

THE FORTH and the CLYDE TOUR Part Two

Routes shown thus:—
8 → 9 → 10 → 11
12 → 13 → 14 →

Stirling
St. Ninians
Kippen
Spout of Ballochleam
Fintry
King's Yetts Rd.
Res.
Meikle Bin
Garrel Burn
Kilsyth
Campsie Glen
Loch Laggan
Balfron
CAMPSIE FELLS
Earl's Seat
Dumgoyne
Blanefield
Strathblane
Finnich Glen
Cameron Muir
Whangie
KILPATRICK HILLS
Loch Lomond
Balloch
Helensburgh
Cardross
R. CLYDE
Erskine Ferry
Bishopton
GARELOCH
LOCH LONG
Gourock
Greenock
Glasgow
FORTH AND CLYDE CANAL

N

7

Road at Randieford Bridge, where the Endrick Water winds its way down from the Spout of Ballochleam. At a point near the bridge, the stream turns at right angles and forms the Loup of Fintry on its way to Loch Lomond.

The River Endrick crosses under the main road to Fintry. A little beyond Walton Bridge is the Loup of Fintry—a water-fall nearly 100 feet in height. Between the falls and the road are the Gowk Stanes, possibly marking the site of some ancient place of entertainment.

The road descends all the time, and after you pass Broomhall Bridge, which crosses Cammel Burn, you are soon in Fintry. You will like this place—there are no railways, few buses and little or no traffic.

Note.—Since the first edition was written a reservoir has been built, covering some of these lands and the face of the country-side has been changed and its beauty added to. The original description of the country-side has purposely not been deleted, but remember, there is a large sheet of water where there was once a bare and lonely moorland. The River Carron flows from the eastern end of the dam. The Endrick Water has not been affected by the building of the dam. The route between Carron Bridge and Fintry runs for most of its length by the side of the reservoir.

Ninth day.

THE SPOUT OF BALLOCHLEAM

Route in brief : Fintry—Randieford Bridge—King's Yetts Road—Cringate Farm—Burnfoot—Spout of Ballochleam—Boquhan Glen—Kippen—Loch Laggan—Fintry.

Walking distance : 12 miles; 19 miles if including the extension.

Map : Ordnance Survey 1″ scale, No. 66.

From Fintry you retrace the road followed yesterday as far as the ruins of Sir John de Grahame's castle on the King's Yetts Road. A little beyond these ruins is a track bearing away to the left, which follows the line of the Endrick. The track is very indistinct in parts, but this need not worry you because you will take the Endrick Water as your guide. About a mile beyond Cringate Farm the stream divides. It is here that the two hill streams of different names meet to give birth to the Endrick. The stream coming down on your right, between the Ling Hill and Cringate Law, is known as the Burnfoot Burn and, near its source in the Gargunnock Hills, as Mary Glyn's Burn. The stream coming down the left-hand side of the Ling Hill is known as the Backside Burn and has its source in the Spout of Ballochleam. On the right-hand side of this stream, along the slopes of the Ling Hill, you will find the track which commences at Burnfoot Burn. This track carries you to the Spout, where the Fintry Hills join the Gargunnock Hills. The crags on the left culminate in Stronend and Skiddaw and to the right there is the Lease Hill and Standmilane Crag. The Boquhan Burn commences at Ballochleam flowing down the gully into the Vale of Kippen to continue through the woodlands to the Forth, a little east of Flanders Moss. This stream makes little impression in the early part of its course, but in the glen proper it cuts its way through the red sandstone, making curious wells and pots. This is particularly noticeable at the Covenanters' Hiding Place in Boquhan Glen. Part of the glen is referred to on the map as The Whale's Belly—why, I have not been able to ascertain. The track down from Ballochleam directs you down to Ballochleam Farm, beyond which you join the main road about half a mile north of Bailie Bow's Bridge. Having reached the main road, turn to the left, and follow the road uphill for about two miles, and so to Kippen, where you should take the opportunity of visiting the famous Kippen Vine.

Tenth day.

THE MEIKLE BIN

Route in brief : Fintry—Crow Road—Meikle Bin—Garrel Glen—Kilsyth.

Walking distance : 12 miles.

Maps : Ordnance Survey 1″ scale, Nos. 68 and 72.

Up the Crow Road out of Fintry you see the Gonachan Glen winding away to the right, while on the left the Tochan Burn follows the line of the road. Across on the open hill-side is Waterhead Farm, with a track coming down to the main road. Follow this track as far as the farm, where you take to the hill-side. The road to Waterhead crosses the River Carron, a tributary of which is the Bin Burn. Follow the Bin Burn for some considerable distance and then make your own way across the moor to the summit of the Meikle Bin. When descending, you will find a track down to the Birken Reservoir, from which follow the Birken Burn to the head of the Garrel Glen, marked by the Laird's Loup. This waterfall does not claim any distinction for its height, but is unusual in that a track leads behind it. Not more than one person at a time is recommended to negotiate this path, otherwise there is a possibility of a soaking. From the water-fall a path leads down the line of the Garrel Glen to Kilsyth. The various place-names in this glen suggest that it has harboured witches and the Devil himself ! There is a De'il's Seat, which is connected with the story of a miller who tried to wrestle with the Devil; the Witches' Linn is another well-known place in the glen, while it is said that those convicted of being witches were drowned in the pool above Allenfauld. At the Allenfauld Bridge turn to the right and rejoin the glen at the next bridge, and finally leave it at the whitewashed mill to join the foot of the Takmadoon Road. Before the coal in the district was exploited, Kilsyth was mainly con-cerned with weaving.

Eleventh day.

THE STRATHBLANE HILLS

Route in brief : Bus to Kilsyth—Campsie Glen (change buses at Kirkintilloch)—Jamie Wright's Well—Fin Glen—Earl's Seat—Ballagan Glen—Blanefield.

Walking distance : 11 miles.

Maps : Ordnance Survey 1″ scale, No. 72, and " The Trossachs and Loch Lomond."

Travel from Kilsyth on the Glasgow bus and alight at Kirkintilloch to change to the bus for Campsie Glen. · In the very short distance from the entrance to the glen to the point where you climb out to the Crow Road, a distance of barely one mile, you have a whole host of queer place-names. First you have the Lady's Linn, in which the Spout of Craiglea jumps down from Maggie Lapsley Knowe formed by the waters of the Aldessan Burn, which rises near the summit of the Hart Hill. The path to follow is on the opposite side of the stream from the Spout of Craiglea where the path follows a tortuous course through a jumble of tumbled rock. So you come to Jacob's Ladder, and waterfalls known as the Wee and Muckle Alicompen. The stream that you are following is known as the Nineteen Times Burn. Often I have enquired the reason for this name, but nobody seems to know it. Some state that the old Crow Road from Lennoxtown to Fintry crosses the stream nineteen times; others maintain that the name comes from the fact that the stream has nineteen tributaries.

At the head of the glen you climb on to the road at a point where Jamie Wright's Well stands by the roadside. A local poet, James M. Slimmon, composed the lines which have been inscribed on the well, and once a year a party of local admirers clean the well, which was erected in 1900. From Jamie Wright's Well you do not follow the road either up or down, but cross the moorland to the west of Allanhead Farm, a whitewashed cottage that stands out distinctly on the hill-side. From there you continue to the line of the Fin Glen, but do not descend to the water-side, instead, continue along the hill-side, in line with the glen. In this way you steadily approach your objective, which is Earl's Seat.

If, however, you wish to go exploring in the glen, there are two fine waterfalls, the Black Spout and the White Spout. These are lower down. The stream following down the Fin Glen is formed by a number of tributaries which rise in the moorland between Earl's Seat and the Corrie of Balglass. You cross the stream and follow the fourth tributary on the left. This will carry you up the eastern slope of Earl's Seat and so to the march fence which shows the way to the summit.

From the summit of Earl's Seat follow the march fence, where it descends in a south-westerly direction, and you will find yourself in the Ballagan Glen. This is a long and bare glen which ends in the Ballagan Spout, a place of particular interest to geologists. On the western side of the Spout a path brings you down to Blanefield. Farther west from Ballagan Spout, along the line of the cliffs, is what is known as the Little Wangie, a cleft of rock which is a small edition of the well-known Whangie in the Kilpatrick Hills. Going still farther west is Jenny's Lum. The name of the Lum commemorates a certain Jenny Brash who was once an inhabitant of Netherton.

Twelfth day.
ACROSS THE CAMERON MUIR

Route in brief : Blanefield—Cuilt Brae—Stockiemuir Road —Finnich Glen—Cameron Muir—Balloch.
Walking distance : 16 miles.
Maps : Same as for the previous day.

At Blanefield Station, the road known as the Cuilt Brae winds uphill across to the main Stockiemuir road. On the way you will see a footpath on the left which leads to Craig-allian Loch. This loch is a particularly bonny sight and you will find it well worth the trouble to make the short detour to have a peep at the wooded loveliness of the district. Back again on the road, you follow on to what is known as the Stockiemuir Road—the main road connecting Glasgow with Drymen—where you turn to the right and, after a little more than a mile of walking, come to the head of the road where Loch Lomond and its attendant mountains are spread out as a background to the wide, sweeping view.

At the foot of the Stockiemuir Road you come to the bridge that crosses Finnich Glen. Look over to the left and you see an interesting gully ; to the right and you look down into an awe-inspiring gorge, dark and dismal, through which the waters make a tortuous way. If you explore the glen you find stepping-stones—Jacob's Ladder—leading down to the Devil's Pulpit in the gorge.

Immediately beyond the bridge, the road climbs up to Finnich Toll, where you turn to the left, along the grassy drove-road that brings you to Jamestown and so to Balloch. This road across the Cameron Muir is the best walk of the day, since for some distance you have a wide and uninterrupted view of Loch Lomond. This view of the loch, with all the islands standing out like gems against the blue of the water, is perhaps the finest of all.

In Balloch you will find accommodation of various sorts offered, although the place caters mainly for the day-tripper. Balloch is a typical trippers' resort, and its main feature is a colony of house-boats anchored in the River Leven between Balloch Bridge and Loch Lomond. Some time ago a factory was erected in the village with the result that the majestic view of Ben Lomond now includes a chimney-stack.

Thirteenth day.

THE STONEYMOLLAN ROAD

Route in brief : Luss Road—Stoneymollan Road—Cardross —Helensburgh.

Walking distance : 7 miles.

Map : Ordnance Survey, special map, " Trossachs and Loch Lomond," or 1″ scale, No. 72.

At the head of Balloch Loan, which you follow from Balloch Station, turn to the right along the main Luss road. About fifty yards along this road you will observe an opening which appears to be a private road. It is, however, the hill road leading across to the Firth of Clyde at a point between Cardross and Helensburgh. The entrance to this road is guarded by a cottage on either side, but no one will dispute your right to come this way. The ascent becomes steeper and, until you reach the turning for Stoneymollan Cottage, you find that your wind is considerably taxed.

The road beyond Stoneymollan Cottage continues uphill to the gate, on the right of which you will see the Cross Stone. This stone is said to be a Bore Stone marking the rallying point of the Clan Colquhoun. Across to the left the fence leads away to the Bromley Muir, from the summit of which there is an extensive view of both Loch Lomond and the Clyde.

Beyond the Cross Stone the road begins to descend, and before long you come in sight of the Clyde, with Greenock and Dunoon clearly visible. The road now winds down by the side of Killoeter, a hill very similar in shape, only much longer, to the Conic Hill rising up from Balmaha. It is said that the Conic Hill and the line of islands in Loch Lomond and Killoeter, form part of the Great Fault. Soon your road brings you down to Cardross at a point opposite the peninsula of Ardmore. You are now on the main road, about three miles from Helensburgh. This road has too much traffic on it to give you any enjoyment from walking and so you are advised to wait for the next bus to take you to your destination.

Fourteenth day.
THE STONE MONKEYS

Route in brief : Boat from Helensburgh to Greenock—Bus to Langbank—Formakin House—Bishopton—Erskine— Erskine Ferry—Bus to Glasgow.

Walking distance : 11 miles.

Map : Ordnance Survey 1″ scale, No. 72.

Travel to Langbank by train or bus and, at the station, follow the by-way that winds uphill to join the high road running parallel to the shore road. Turn to the left along this parallel road and, after about half a mile of walking, you come to the road-junction at Ferryhill Plantation. On your left is a road leading down to Langbank; on your right is a by-way winding uphill, through the farmyard of Netherton, to skirt Barscube Hill. Follow this uphill track and, after passing through Netherton Farm, you reach a point where woodlands edge the side of the road. A gap in these woodlands gives a view of the lochans on the estate of Drums. On your left the slopes of Barscube Hill rise steeply and invite you to climb to the summit. When descending, come down to the road you have left and continue in the same direction. This brings you to the back road leading to Houston. At this road, turn to the right to come to Barochan. Turning to the left along this main road you come to the Mill of Barochan, where the path branches away to the right to wander through Swines Glen; it is a pretty path, but there is more of interest ahead, so leave Swines Glen for another visit.

Continuing along the main road you turn to the right, downhill, to come to the mill and the House of Formakin. The entrance gates to this house are said to be replicas of the gates of Newgate Prison. On the summit of each of the two turrets of the lodge are statuettes of monkeys, but a unique sight is presented at the stables, where groups of stone monkeys can be seen on the roof. Beyond Formakin House the road winds uphill and brings you to the House of Gatehead, which stands a little back from the road on its own small carriage-drive. Your road leads past the house and on to the main road that connects Greenock with Glasgow. Cross this road and follow the by-way called Chestnut Walk, at the end of which turn to the right, then, almost immediately, to the left, whence you have two miles of walking and through the small village of Erskine to Erskine Ferry. The monument on the left-hand side of the road, approaching Erskine, was erected to the memory of the Lord of Blantyre. Beyond the village the track leads away to Bargaran, where a famous witch is said to have lived. This is referred to in *Witchcraft Annals* as the scene of the tragedy of Bargaran's daughter in 1697, and that is described as one of the last trials for witchcraft in Arnott's collection of *Criminal Trials*. It is gathered from this report that five persons were executed in connection with the affair.

At the end of the road from Erskine you turn to the left, and come to the ferry across the Clyde. At the other side of the river you are on the main Dumbarton–Glasgow road, where a frequent service of buses connects with Glasgow.

VI

THE SEVENTEEN LOCHS

INTRODUCTION

THIS tour starts at Hunter's Quay, near Dunoon, on the Firth of Clyde, and introduces the tramper to some of the finest scenery in Scotland. Every type that Scotland has to offer is included—bens and glens, lochs and forests. Beginning on the west coast, the tour carries one to the doorstep of the east coast, and finishes up in the heart of the Western Highlands, where there is the opportunity of seeing something of the Grampians. At the end of the fortnight those who wish can quite well travel on to Edinburgh and spend some time in that fair city.

First day.

Travel from Central Station, Glasgow, *via* Gourock to Hunter's Quay, or from Queen Street Station, Glasgow, *via* Craigendoran to Hunter's Quay.

Second day.

BISHOP'S SEAT AND GLEN KIN

Route in brief : Hunter's Quay—Dunoon—Victoria Parade—Balgie Burn—Kilbride Road—The Reservoirs—The Pass of the Humming Noise—Glen Kin—Glen Lean—The Holy Loch—Sandbank.

Walking distance : 15 miles.

Map : Ordnance Survey, special map, " Firth of Clyde."

From Hunter's Quay, follow the sea-front through Kirn to Dunoon. The road follows the line of the West Bay along the sea-front to the Balgie Burn, at which point you leave the sea to turn up Kilbride Road. Before turning up this road,

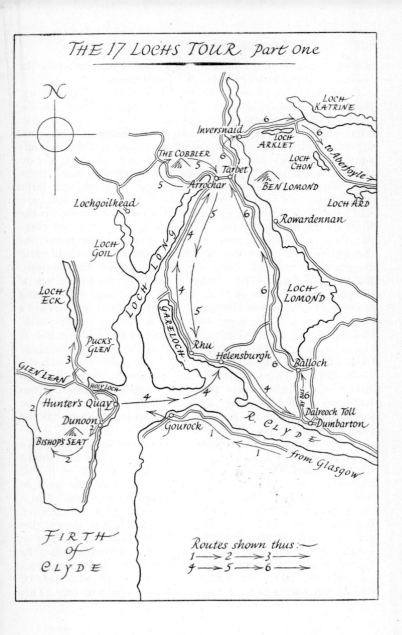

THE 17 LOCHS TOUR Part One

Routes shown thus :—
1 → 2 → 3 →
4 → 5 → 6 →

FIRTH of CLYDE

however, you should continue for a short distance along the front to visit the beautiful Morag's Fairy Glen.

From Kilbride Road turn to the left to the reservoirs. Next, follow the path up to the right and continue up the slope to the top reservoir. Looking back the way you have come you have a magnificent view of the series of reservoirs, together with an extensive view of the Clyde and the uplands south of Gourock and Greenock. Near at hand is the stream that feeds the reservoirs; follow it on the right-hand bank and, after a short distance, make your objective the large pole at the rifle range. A little above, and on the left, you will observe a deep gully; follow it up and continue up the slope of the hill to the top, where there is a stretch of comparatively flat land beyond which a steeper slope rises. At the top of this you come to what is called The Badd, and congratulate yourself that you have reached the summit. But you have not. The summit is away across to the left of the peat-hags and boggy bits. Do not be content with having reached The Badd, but continue to climb to the top of Bishop's Seat, where the most impressive view is the one to the south, looking down Strath Eachaig to Loch Eck. The scene is alpine in its grandeur, for the mountains appear to rise sheer from Loch Eck which is connected by a green vale with the Holy Loch. Turning south-west you look across Bute to Arran. The three lochs stretching across the island from Rothesay to Scalpsie Bay appear to be as one and to be joined to the sea at the far end, giving an impression that the Island of Bute is two islands.

From Bishop's Seat descend, in a northerly direction, to the walls of Glen Kin, whence you bear to the left to come to what is called The Giant's Knowe; skirt the top of it and continue to the watershed, which is marked on the map as Bealach na Srèine—The Pass of the Humming Noise. From the head of the pass you have a splendid view right down Inverchaolain Glen. Do not, however, follow down this glen, but turn around and go right down Glen Kin. If you would like some pleasant scrambling, come back to the Giant's Knowe and scramble down the gully. Continue down the glen and, at the woodlands, keep to the left-hand side of the stream and make for the farmhouse you will see. This farmhouse is connected with the outside world by a good metalled road. At the road-end turn to the right and, after a mile of walking down Glen Lean, you come to the Holy Loch at Dalinlongart, which is about one mile from Sandbank. If you wish, you have the opportunity of travelling by bus to Sandbank and Hunter's Quay, but it is a very pleasant road for walking.

Third day.

A DAY IN THE STATE FOREST

A separate chapter has been devoted to the Argyll National Forest Park and you should refer to the pages concerned for further information.

On the fifth day of this tour you will be walking on the estate of the Forest Park and to-day you have the opportunity of visiting Puck's Glen on the estate and also the forest nurseries at Benmore House where the Forestry office and school are situated. There is a bus service from Dunoon to Puck's Glen during the season and also there is an all-the-year–round service, Dunoon-Ardentinny, which you could use. Should you do so, alight at the Eachaig Bridge when you have a short walk through the strath to come to the glen.

A useful all-day excursion embracing Puck's Glen and the Forestry nurseries is as follows: Travel by the Dunoon-Ardentinny service bus as far as Eachaig Bridge, and then walk the Strath Eachaig road for about a mile until you come to the entrance to Puck's Glen, which is on the right-hand side of the road. There is a well-made track that runs uphill through the glen to Puck's House, and beyond to where the track takes you by another route, even more delightful, back to the road at a point not far from where you entered. Continue along the road in the direction in which you were going at the time you entered the glen. Soon you will come to the entrance gates for Benmore House on your left and here you can enquire about admission times.

If, by the time you make your expedition, the Forestry Commission has provided an access route from the head of Puck's Glen to the open hill-side, it is recommended that you visit the nurseries first and then go on to the glen. You could then continue on to the open hill, have your lunch there, and cross the high ground, *via* Craigmore Wood, to the forest road which leads down to Gairletter on Loch Long side.   From that point you could return by the Ardentinny–Dunoon service bus.   If, on the other hand, there is no access path from the head of Puck's Glen, return on foot to Eachaig Bridge and continue by the Ardentinny bus as far as Gairletter on Loch Long side.   Follow the forest road from Gairletter to the hill and then make your own way towards Strone Point and descend through the golf course to the village of Strone at the junction of Loch Long and the Holy Loch.   You can then return to Dunoon or Hunter's Quay by the Ardentinny–Dunoon service bus.

Fourth day.
TO HELENSBURGH

Before the war there was a ferry service between Rosneath and Rhu that enabled you to leave the boat at Kilcreggan and enjoy a pleasant walk on the Rosneath peninsula and finish by crossing to Rhu and walking the short distance to Helensburgh.   At the time of writing, the ferry is not operating; perhaps it will be resumed later on.   If you are going this way you will need to walk about half-way up the loch-side before you would come to a ferry.   Conditions are changed in these days on Gare Loch side and there is not the same attraction for the country lover.   Faslane Bay is now a ship-breaking yard and is not a place where one would wish to linger except on business.   The best thing you can do, therefore, is to travel from Dunoon to Craigendoran on the steamer.   At some later date the railway company may change the route, but at present the boat on this run crosses the firth to Gourock before making for Craigendoran; it is an ideal arrangement for the holiday-maker, for it gives a longer voyage and a better opportunity of seeing the shipping in the river.

Many of the Clyde steamers are back again on their old runs after their war services, and though some of the well-known boats will never come back, those that have returned look very neat and clean in their peace-time dress.

At Craigendoran you connect with the Highland Railway

for Arrochar, where you should stay overnight in readiness for the Cobbler climb the next day.

An alternative is to leave the boat at Kilcreggan; turn to the right after leaving the pier and walk along the main road for three miles to come to Rosneath. From here you follow the road on the west side of the Gare Loch up to Whistlefield. You could stay the night here or, if the train connection is suitable, continue by train to Arrochar.

Fifth day.

CLIMBING THE COBBLER

Route in brief: Arrochar Station—Arrochar Village—Torpedo Station—Sourmilk Burn—Summit of The Cobbler.

Walking distance : One mountain.

Map : Ordnance Survey, special map, " Trossachs and Loch Lomond."

Travel by train to Arrochar. At the foot of the station approach, turn to the right for a mile of walking to Arrochar village. Proceed through the village to the head of the loch where the Two Shires' Bridge carries the road over the stream. This bridge stands at the head of Glen Loin. Here stands the Arrochar Youth Hostel; it is near its site that the " Rucksack Hut " was erected, which had the distinction of being the first building erected for that purpose in Great Britain.

From the Two Shires' Bridge, follow the road to the far side of the loch and on as far as the Torpedo Station. Here you see the foaming Sourmilk Burn making its way into the loch. This stream will be your guide to reach the summit of The Cobbler. It is not necessary to give you directions for the rest of the walk until you reach the head of the stream. By this time you will have the massive top of The Cobbler clearly in view. At the appropriate time you will know when to leave the stream and negotiate the rugged peak. The real thrill comes at the top—a mass of rock which marks the ultimate summit. To reach the top of this rock you must creep through a hole; make your way along a narrow ledge and so up to the top.

Like most hills, The Cobbler can be very dangerous in mist and you are recommended to call off this excursion unless there is good visibility. It will be disappointing if you do not obtain a good view from the summit as you are in the midst of a whole regiment of heights, most of which are between 2,000 feet and 3,000 feet. Ben Lomond seems very near at hand and, almost next door in another direction, you see Beinn Ime, which is even higher than Ben Lomond.

A convenient stream will be found a short distance from the top of The Cobbler and, after your lunch, you have a steady walk downhill back to the loch-side and to your train at Arrochar.

Sixth day.

WALKING TO THE TROSSACHS

Route in brief : Helensburgh to Dumbarton—Balloch—Loch Lomond—Stronachlachar—Loch Chon—Loch Ard—Aberfoyle.

Walking distance : 15 miles.

Map : Ordnance Survey 1″ special map, " The Trossachs."

Travel by the Glasgow bus as far as Dalreoch Toll, just at the entrance to the town of Dumbarton. At the road-junction change to the Balloch bus, and time your arrival to enable you to connect with the morning boat at Balloch pier for Inversnaid. Balmaha is one of the favourite picnicking places with out-of-doors lovers and is very busy at week-ends. From Balmaha the boat cuts across the loch again to Luss and this time winds in and out of the many islands, the chief of which are Inchfad, Inchmoan, Inchconnachan and Inchtavannach; so to Luss and then across the loch up to Rowardennan. Here you would alight if you intended to climb Ben Lomond. If you do so, you can descend the northern face to Comer and back to the road at " The Tea Pot " on the road to Aberfoyle. The route up Ben Lomond is clearly defined all the way. For the road to Comer you must descend the steep northern face and bear slightly to the east all the time. In this way you will come to the farmhouse of Comer at the head of the Black Glen. Having reached this farmhouse you find a track leading down the glen to the Aberfoyle road at a point between Loch Chon and Loch Ard.

LOCH ACHRAY

BEN VORLICH AND LOCH EARN

Robert M. Adam

If it is not your intention to climb Ben Lomond, continue on the steamer up to Inversnaid, where you begin your walk to the Trossachs. From the pier the road winds steeply uphill and carries through Glen Arklet, by the side of Loch Arklet, to Stronachlachar on Loch Katrine. Both Loch Arklet and Loch Katrine are part of the Glasgow waterworks scheme.

From Loch Katrine side retrace your steps a short distance and then turn to the left, along the Aberfoyle road. A little more than two miles of walking along this moorland road and you descend slightly to come to Loch Chon. Then you come to the Black Lochan and go on by way of the Water of Chon to Loch Ard. Out of Loch Ard flows the River Forth.

A short distance after leaving the Black Lochan you come to the little clachan of " The Tea Pot " where, for a number of years, Mrs. Black gave kindly hospitality. She now lives at Kinlochard Post Office. The Rucksack Hut at Kinlochard, a converted bothy, was the first Youth Hostel in Scotland.

For a distance of a mile the road hugs the water's edge and then leads to Aberfoyle, your destination for the night.

Seventh day.

A DAY ON THE ISLAND OF REST

Route in brief : Walk along the Stirling Road to Port of Menteith—Ferry across the Lake to Inchmahome—The Island of Rest—Visit the monastery on the Island—Return the same way to Aberfoyle.

Walking distance : 8 miles.

Map : Ordnance Survey 1″ special map, " Trossachs."

Walk or bus to the Port of Menteith and the lake. The ferryman, who still retains a Cockney accent, will tell you all and more about the old priory on the Island of Inchmahome. Inchmahome, or the Island of Rest, is the larger of two islands in this, the only lake in Scotland. It is definitely marked as a lake on the Ordnance Survey maps, but the *Statistical Account* and a book entitled the *Lakes of Scotland*, published in 1836, both refer to it as Menteith Loch. The other, or smaller,

8

island immediately to the east, is called the Island of Talla or the Earl's Isle. There is another very small island referred to as the Dog Isle, possibly because of the fact that the one-time Earls of Menteith used this as their dog-kennel. The old priory on the Island of Inchmahome was founded by Walter Cumyng, Earl of Menteith who, in 1238, obtained the authority of the Bishops of Glasgow and Dunkeld in the name of the Pope for building the church of Inchmaquhomock. Beyond the island is the peninsula called Cnoc n'an Bocan—Hob Goblin Hill.

Long ago, in the days when people believed in fairies, the Earl of Menteith owned the " Red Book." To open this book was to be subject to certain penalties from the wee folk. One of the family opened the book and immediately the fairies demanded that they should be given work, so he set them the task of building a road to the island. They began on the southern side and built a peninsula, but at this moment the Earl stopped them and set them the task of making a rope of sand. They struck work at that point and resolved to depart. The Earl was so glad to be rid of them that the fairies were given the northern shoulder of Ben Venue (Coire na Uriusgean), the Cave of the Fairies.

For the return journey you have an alternative to the main road. Shortly after you have left the lake you come to a little by-way at Malling. This by-way takes you across the low-lying ground to Windygate at Gartmore Station. Cross the bridge away from Aberfoyle and follow up the hill towards the village of Gartmore, but, after about a quarter of a mile, turn to the right to follow the path across to Easter Park, and so in at the back door to Aberfoyle.

Eighth day.

THE TROSSACHS

Route in brief : Duke's Road—Loch Achray—Loch Katrine —Brig o' Turk—Duke's Road—Aberfoyle.

Walking distance : 15 miles.

Map : Ordnance Survey 1″ special map, " Trossachs."

The town of Aberfoyle makes an excellent centre for excursions in all directions since, in whatever direction you set

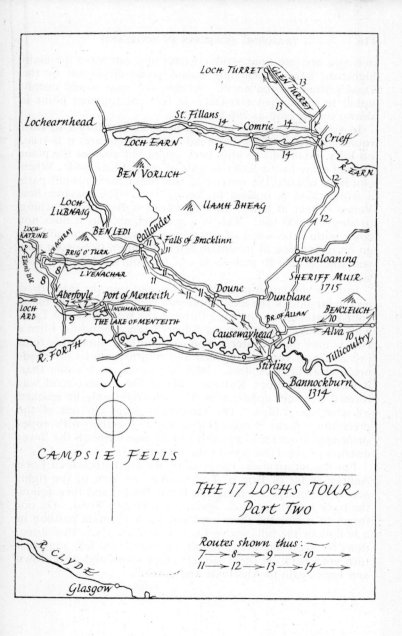

LOCH TURRET
GLEN TURRET
13
13
Lochearnhead
St. Fillans 14 Comrie 14
LOCH EARN 14
Crieff
R. EARN
BEN VORLICH
12
UAMH BHEAG
12
LOCH LUBNAIG
LOCH KATRINE
LOCH ACHRAY
BEN LEDI
Callander
11 Falls of Bracklinn
11
ELLEN'S ISLE
8
BRIG O' TURK
L. VENACHAR
8
11
Greenloaning
SHERIFF MUIR 1715
Aberfoyle Port of Menteith
7 7
INCHMAHOME
11 Doune
11
Dunblane
LOCH ARD
9
THE LAKE OF MENTEITH
BR. OF ALLAN
BENCLEUCH 10
11
Causewayhead
Alva 10
Tillicoultry
R. FORTH
9 9
10
9
Stirling
N
Bannockburn 1314

CAMPSIE FELLS

THE 17 LOCHS TOUR
Part Two

Routes shown thus :—
7 → 8 → 9 → 10 →
11 → 12 → 13 → 14 →

R. CLYDE
Glasgow

out, you are into your stride at once and can leave the main high-road behind. On this occasion you climb out by the Duke's Road to the north. At first the road winds steeply uphill to more than 600 feet; in fact the topmost point is shown on the map as 796 feet.

In your eagerness to stem the brae, do not forget to turn round and enjoy the widespread view. There are, it is true, no lofty mountains to look back upon, but you see the plain leading away to the lesser heights of central Scotland. When you have reached the watershed and begin the downhill path a wonderland is opened up before you. The massive Ben Venue is near at hand; directly ahead is Ben Ledi reaching to almost 3,000 feet. This is a grand climb, but it does not come within the scope of this tour. It would be possible to go on telling you of mountain after mountain to be seen, but you will be able to pick them out for yourself by the aid of your map.

In time you come to Loch Achray and join the main road on the far side of the loch where you turn to the left, to make your pilgrimage by the road through the woodlands, to Loch Katrine side. The famous Silver Strand, opposite Ellen's Isle, is now under water. You can continue along this road just as far as you feel inclined and return again to the road-junction at Loch Achray. Nowadays it is much easier than it was to visit Loch Katrine. Before the present road was formed it would appear that the loch could only be reached by what was called "The Ladders"—steps cut out of the precipitous rocky bank. These steps, together with ropes suspended from trees, enabled you to pass through the lower districts of the Trossachs to the higher parts.

For the return walk, travel along the northern side of Loch Achray as far as Brig o' Turk where you turn to the right, across the bridge spanning the Black Water, and then follow the track uphill and back again to the Duke's Road. Do not forget to notice the three-cornered Loch Drunkie nestling in a hollow of the hills above Loch Venachar. No other directions for the route are required, but when you feel you must turn your back on the Trossachs, face south and walk down and back again to Aberfoyle and dinner.

Ninth day.

STIRLING

Route in brief : Morning bus to Stirling—Afternoon, visit the Wallace Monument and Stirling Castle.

Map : Ordnance Survey 1″ scale, No. 67.

This is a day of rest, a day on which you will have the opportunity of visiting the historic town of Stirling, a busy tourist junction on the main road from central Scotland to the Highlands. Having passed through Stirling one feels that the threshold of Scotland's real scenery has been crossed. When travelling to Stirling on the Edinburgh bus you have a magnificent view of the town together with its surrounding amphitheatre of hills. When you come to the hospital outside the town, if you have visited Salzburg in Austria, you will see a striking similarity in the view. The rock on which Stirling Castle stands can be likened to the citadel of Salzburg, and there is also a great resemblance in the background of mountains.

From the ramparts of the Castle you see the Ochil Hills, while the winding Forth unfolds like a silver ribbon on its tortuous course to the sea; the Pentland Hills, green to the top, carry your eyes to the south, and across from the ramparts you can see the Lady's Rock on which there is a mountain-view indicator. Copies of the chart can be obtained from the local booksellers. Across from the Castle you see the Wallace Monument standing up against the sky-line on the crags above Causewayhead. There is a circular staircase inside the tower that leads to a platform on the summit. On each of the four sides of the platform there is a chart showing you the names of all the places to be seen.

Tenth day.

BENCLEUCH—THE TWENTY-ONE COUNTIES' VIEW

Route in brief: Stirling—Tillicoultry—Tillicoultry Glen—Bencleuch—Alva Glen—Stirling.

Walking distance : One mountain.

Map : Ordnance Survey 1″ scale, No. 67.

Travel by bus from Stirling to Tillicoultry and book a return ticket. Tillicoultry is a convenient starting-point for the ascent of Bencleuch (2,363 feet), the highest hill in the Ochils, from which the most extensive and beautiful views in the country can be obtained. The ravine in Tillicoultry Glen has been opened to the public by the formation of a well-constructed track from which paths lead to the hills. The opening up of the glen was the result of hard work given by the local people under the leadership of Provost Jamieson.

Some years ago a number of local people, resident in Toronto, subscribed sufficient money to erect a view indicator, to be placed on the slopes of Tillicoultry Glen. In due course it was arranged that a mountain-view indicator should be erected on the summit of Bencleuch. A chart for this indicator was prepared by Mr. D. K. Paterson who prepared the Ben Lomond and Goat Fell charts. In the preparation of these maps he was assisted by the Ordnance Survey Department and by Mr. Mathieson of the Royal Geographical Society of Edinburgh. All the material for this chart was carried to the summit by the local people, who gave willingly of their time and labour.

The road to the glen leads up from the main street, and the path through the glen climbs steeply by leaping waterfalls, meanders through leafy glades and, finally, climbs out of the glen from the reservoir. Having left the glen you will find a path that breasts the hill and carries you to the stream of the Daiglen. The track then follows the right-hand side of the Daiglen and ignores the Inner Burn. The second tributary is called the Outer Burn and you find that the path leads uphill on the left of this stream bringing you up on the ridge west of Bencleuch. Follow the march fence eastwards when you will come to the cairn and the indicator on the summit. There are 119 vantage points marked on this plan, showing places in twenty-one counties. The outline of the coast and certain towns are shown, but it is not possible to see them; every mountain shown, however, can definitely be seen.

For the descent, follow the march fence to the west and then, at the fence junction, follow the fence going downhill on your left. This fence brings you to the watershed that divides the Daiglen and Glenwinnel. This is your way, and at the foot of the hill a well-defined footpath brings you along the western slopes of Ben Ever. After a while this path leads out of Glenwinnel through the gap to Ben Ever and the Nebit, to bring you into Alva by way of the Silver Glen. Do not follow this path, however, into the Silver Glen; instead, keep along the western slope of the Nebit and follow the Glenwinnel Burn down to where it leaps to join the Alva Burn. Across the Alva Burn you find a properly defined path that will take you to Alva.

Note.—The indicator-chart at the summit of Bencleuch was removed as a war-time precaution, but was replaced on June 13, 1948.

Eleventh day.

BRACKLINN FALLS

Route in brief : Train or bus to Callander—Bracklinn Falls —Callander—Falls of Leny—Loch Lubnaig—Callander.

Walking distance : 9 miles.

Map : Ordnance Survey 1″ special map, " Trossachs."

At the station entrance, facing towards the hotel, turn to the left and follow over the railway bridge to continue along the by-road. A notice points the way to the Bracklinn Falls and the path leads uphill through a sea of flaming yellow gorse. Before long you come to diverging routes; one path leads to the road, while the other leads to the waterfall. Following the path to the waterfall you come to a deep cleft down which the Keltie Water runs from the near-by moorland. There is a bridge across the swirling waters erected at the finest vantage point. When the stream is in spate you have a vivid impression of wild, untamed power venting its rage on the rocks beneath. On the way back visit the Red Well, restored by the Callander Amenity Committee in April 1924. When returning to Callander, wander through the woods and climb to the top of the Crags where a view of the surrounding country is presented. Immediately below, you see the town hugging the River Teith, while, all around, is a smiling country-side which has been the scene of many an invasion, from the days of the Romans to those of the present-day tourists. On the shoulder of Ben Ledi (The Hill of God), which stands out clear and bold, is a small lochan—The Small Lake of the Dead Bodies. From the legend connected with this loch it would appear that some two hundred persons were journeying from Glen Finlas to the churchyard in the Pass of Leny. Their route brought them to this loch and, finding the water frozen over and covered with snow, they attempted to cross it, but the ice gave way and all were drowned.

From the crags above Callander you will also see the waters of Loch Venachar. It is said that, within this lake, a monster, known as the Wild Horse of Killievronie, lived. This beast was supposed to tempt children to take a ride on its back and then carry them to destruction in the heart of the lake.

After descending to the town, if time permits, you should follow the north road out of Callander to visit the Leny Falls, beyond which is Loch Lubnaig.

Twelfth day.
ACROSS SHERIFFMUIR TO CRIEFF

Route in brief: Logie Church from Stirling—Menstrie Glen—Sheriffmuir—Greenloaning—Crieff.

Walking distance: 10 miles.

Maps: Ordnance Survey 1″ scale, Nos. 63 and 67.

Travel by the Tillicoultry bus from Stirling and alight at the connecting road for Logie Church, in Menstrie Glen. You have already been introduced to two of the glens in the Ochils—Tillicoultry and Alva. This, the third of its glens, is not so awe-inspiring, but nevertheless it is a bonny walk and all too soon you climb out of its leafy loveliness to come to the hill road across Sheriffmuir. A Highlander at the battle of Sheriffmuir claimed to have lost his " faither, twa brithers and a gude black belt that was mair worth than them a'."

A little more than a mile along the road you will see a track bearing away to the right, *via* the Clackmannanshire reservoir, and leading right down the eastern side of Menstrie Glen. This route, however, is not the way for to-day. Another mile and a half of walking will bring you to Sheriffmuir Hotel where, at the junction of your road and the road turning down to the left to Dunblane, the Battle of Sheriffmuir is said to have been fought. A further mile and a half of walking and you come to the road on the left which takes you down to Greenloaning. All the way along the road, after reaching the topmost point beyond Sheriffmuir Hotel, you march with your face to the Perthshire heights. Between yourself and those mountains you have the Strath Earn which you cross by motor bus to come to your destination at Crieff. When you reach Greenloaning you await the Crieff bus, for, as you will see from your map, this road is long and uninteresting for the walker and is best negotiated in some other fashion. Passing through Braco you notice, across to your right, the famous Carsebreck Loch where the hopes of thousands of curlers are centred every year. It is said that whenever a bonspiel is arranged a thaw is sure to set in.

You come to Crieff in the early evening and, to complete the day, you should climb the famous Knock Hill. There are many beautiful walks through the woods to the summit. A mountain-view indicator was erected on the Knock Hill before the war and the chart for this was prepared by Mr. D. K. Paterson of Paisley.

Thirteenth day.

LOCH TURRET

Route in brief : Lochearnhead road to Dalvreck—The Blue Craigs—Loch Turret—Falls of Turret—Dalvreck—Crieff.
Walking distance : 12 miles.
Map : Ordnance Survey 1″ scale, No. 63.

From Crieff follow the Lochearnhead road for a distance of one mile when you will come to a turning on your right, at Dalvreck. This road leads you to the heart of the hills. After a short distance the road takes a sharp bend to the right at the Clachan of Hosh and, a few yards after turning to the right, you follow the by-way on the left that leads you to Glen Turret. You will now have the Turret Water on your left-hand side and, after a short distance, you will find that one of its tributaries, the Barvick, joins it immediately before the road you are on crosses the Barvick Burn. You turn to the right along a leafy by-way with the woodlands on the left. Follow this track up to Stonefield Farm and from this farm take to the open hill-side, keeping in line with the Barvick Burn. Your way now is to follow this stream right up to its source. Ere long you will enter a corrie with Creag Chaisean on one side and Stonefield Hill on the other. You should have no difficulty here because all the contours lead you into this corrie, and at the head are the Blue Craigs which you have to negotiate. They will present little difficulty, but you should remember to be well shod. The stream that you are following goes down from these crags and cuts through a break in the middle. You, too, will be able to go through and come to the top of the crags. At this high vantage point you find yourself in a jumble of Highland heights, most of which are over 2,000 feet. Near at hand, across the head of Glen Turret, you will see rocky Ben Chonzie, which just manages to attain the 3,000-feet level at 3,048 feet. The descent to Loch Turret side is steep in parts and the best plan is to follow the stream marked on the map as Allt Choinneachain. This stream brings you down to the track that follows the line of the Turret Water and then you follow all the way down the glen and rest at the Falls of Turret. Finally, you meander through the woodlands at the mouth of Glen Turret, to come back to the Clachan of Hosh, where your road home is clearly defined. On this excursion your view to the north will not be particularly extensive, but to the south you will see right across Strath Earn to the Ochil Hills.

Fourteenth day.

LOCH EARN

Route in brief : Comrie—Loch Earn—Comrie—Dalginross —Strath Earn—Crieff.

Walking distance : 12 miles.

Map : Ordnance Survey 1″ scale, No. 67.

Travel by bus to St. Fillans at Loch Earn. At Loch Earn you may be tempted to linger and laze, and possibly to sail up the loch to Lochearnhead, which stands at the entrance to Glen Ogle where the road leads over to Killin and Loch Tay. After you have lazed and enjoyed the beauties of Loch Earn follow the main road from St. Fillans to the Halt two and a half miles from the village. You then turn to the right, along the by-way through the Ross woodlands and so into Comrie, but again shun the main road. Turn to the right to

Dalginross and then to the left again to follow the road, near to the winding River Earn, to come to Strowan House. Another three miles of walking brings you back to Crieff—and so ends your two weeks of tramping through Central Scotland.

VII

THE WESTERN HIGHLANDS

TO

THE FIRTH OF FORTH

INTRODUCTION

THIS is a continuation of the Skye and Western Highland tour and covers on foot parts of the route you travel by train when going to Oban. It is so easy to say that this, or any tour for that matter, is the finest of the lot, but it would be easy to use up all the available superlatives in praise of this tour and then not do it justice. You have a very wide variety of scenery, a change of programme every day, inland lochs and arms of the sea, towering bens and glowering glens, smiling pastures and barren hill-sides and, finally, the city of Edinburgh as a grand climax to the tour. When you have seen Princes Street, Edinburgh, you have seen the finest street in Europe.

No rest days have been shown in the itinerary, but it will be noticed that only twelve days' touring have been described. This will enable you to fit in your rest days as, and where, you wish. You may wish to put in a day's sailing from Oban, or linger at Stirling, or spend an additional day in Edinburgh. Certainly the latter city will take more than a fleeting visit to do it justice. An extra day, therefore, at the end of a tour can be used very profitably.

First day.

Travel to Oban.

Second day.

GLEN LONAN

Route in brief: Oban—Golf Course—Loch Nell—Glen Lonan—Taynuilt.

Walking distance : 12 miles.

Map : Ordnance Survey 1″ scale, special map, " Oban."

There is no preliminary bus or train journey for this excursion; you start walking right away. Cross the golf course and join the road just before the point where the railway crosses over it. Continue under the railway bridge and then, not very far away, and passing the lochan on your left, the road bears round a wide bend, also to the left. A footpath on the right, however, cuts off the corner and then, at the point where you rejoin the road, you see a side-road facing you from the footpath. This road brings you down to a stream connected to Loch Nell and it is this stream which you follow through the narrow Glen Lonan all the way down to Taynuilt. You have about nine miles of walking through this glen, but it is a quiet road to follow, for motor traffic to and from Oban follows the main road and leaves the Glen Lonan road to those who are content to be more leisurely.

The glen narrows considerably in places, the hills on either side rising up to more than 2,000 feet. The river, too, widens and narrows as it makes a way through the valley, and at one place forms a small loch.

About three or four miles from Taynuilt the glen breaks up, and the road keeps to the side of the hill for a while, then seems to go any old way, sometimes up and sometimes down until, at last, it reaches Taynuilt.

There is no reason why you should start this walk until after lunch and so, during the morning, you have the opportunity to visit Ganavan Sands. The road follows the line of the bay for a good mile and you see, across to the left, the Isle of Kerrera. Then, as you approach Ganavan there is a view across the Firth to the Isle of Lismore. The golden sands of Ganavan invite you to stay but you can, if you wish, include a visit to Dunstaffnage Castle.

Third day.

THE PASS OF BRANDER

Route in brief : Taynuilt — Bridge of Nant — Bridge of Awe—Pass of Brander—Falls of Cruachan—Glen Strae—Dalmally.

Walking distance : 14 miles.

Map : Ordnance Survey 1″ scale, No. 61.

Before starting the day's excursion proper, go by the road, beyond the railway station, which leads right to the shores of Loch Etive. It is good to make a closer acquaintance with this very lovely glen. There is no road along the shores of this long sea loch, although there is a road from the head of the loch, through Glen Etive, to the Moor of Rannoch.

After this brief diversion, leave Taynuilt by the main road to the Pass of Brander. Gradually you perceive that the stream is widening, that the walls of the glen are closing in ; and then you realise that the river is no longer a river—it has become Loch Awe. It is not the largest loch in Scotland—that distinction belongs to Loch Lomond—but it is the longest. You are in the pass by now and the road and the railway struggle to keep a foothold on the steep slopes of Ben Cruachan. It is a pleasant road on which to walk, with magnificent scenery all the way, improving as the view of the loch widens.

You come to the Falls of Cruachan, about half-way through the pass, and then the road sweeps round to the head of Glen Strae and so away from the loch towards Dalmally.

And now you have an alternative worthy of mention. It will involve a greater amount of walking, but will give you a road less popular with motor traffic.

Get out your Oban map. Now look for the road that twists its way up Glen Nant and so to the uplands. It looks a good road, and it is a good road, but it is up to you to choose which of the routes you prefer. However, make sure, before setting out, that the Loch Awe ferry for Port Sonachan is operating. If it is not then it is no use trying to go by this way. If it is, then you can go to Kilchrennan, and on to the end of the road at the North Port on the shores of Loch Awe. There is (or was) a special signalling device at

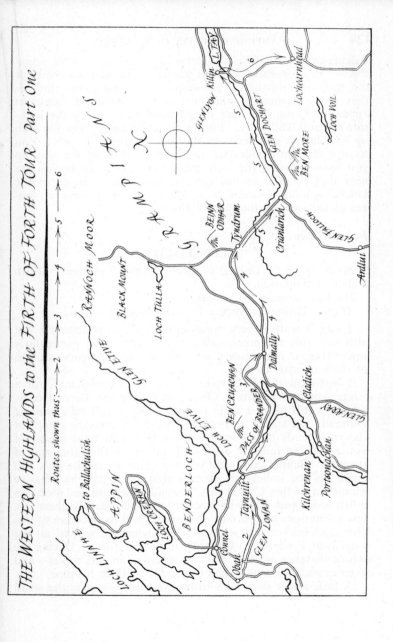

THE WESTERN HIGHLANDS to the FIRTH OF FORTH TOUR Part One

Routes shown thus :— → 2 → 3 → 4 → 5 → 6

Kilchrennan for calling the ferryman across from Port Sonachan. You operated a hand klaxon horn and watched for the ferryman through a telescope. The important thing is that you continue to operate the horn until the boatman appears. Cross over and then follow the road by the lochside towards Dalmally. Follow the road away from the loch up to Cladich and back to the loch beyond Cladich. You have a few more miles yet to Dalmally, but all the way up you have views of the loch and, at the point where you are near that peculiar monument erected to the memory of the Gaelic scholar, Duncan Ban MacIntyre, you have an unparalleled view up the Pass of Brander.

Fourth day.

GLEN LOCHY

Route in brief : Dalmally—Glen Lochy—Tyndrum—Strath Fillan—Crianlarich.
Walking distance : 17 miles.
Maps : Ordnance Survey 1″ scale, Nos. 61 and 62.

To-day's walk is very much in contrast to yesterday's, but although this seventeen-mile tramp may not be particularly interesting, it is necessary to connect one very good section of the tour with another.

You follow the main road east from Dalmally and, for a while, you are in Strath Orchy, alongside the River Orchy, which is still quite a wide stream. About two miles out of Dalmally the strath bears away to the left into the glen, but the road leads into bare Glen Lochy. You have ahead of you about ten miles of road to Tyndrum at the other end of the glen. Behind you—and you must stop to admire now and again—is the collection of hills that make up the massive mountain of Ben Cruachan. The hills rise bare and steep on either side, and you will meet few people because there are few habitations hereabouts. My most vivid recollection of this glen goes back a few years to a day when we walked all the way from Tyndrum to Dalmally in a snowstorm. During the whole distance we met but one person, an old tinker—and even in such a storm he had to ask for a fill for his pipe.

A little under two miles from Tyndrum you pass the small

OBAN BAY

GLEN DOCHART

Lochan na Bi on your right and then comes the junction with the road from the Moor of Rannoch at the village of Tyndrum.

You are now in Strath Fillan with a little less than four miles of walking down this wide, and not so desolate, valley to come to Crianlarich. There is a deep pool in Strath Fillan known as the Holy Pool. Here, in olden times, insane people were dipped in the hope of a cure.

The scenery of Strath Fillan is softer and less wild than that of Glen Lochy and, as you approach Crianlarich, there is more cultivation. Crianlarich is an important road and rail junction. Road and rail join from the south-west, *via* Glen Falloch, with road and rail from the south-east, *via* Glen Dochart.

There is an hotel, cottage accommodation and a youth hostel.

Fifth day.

GLEN DOCHART

Route in brief : Crianlarich—Glen Dochart—Killin.
Walking distance : 14 miles.
Map : Ordnance Survey 1″ scale, No. 62.

Glen Dochart provides you with a wide variety of scenery. Instructions for the journey need be few. At Crianlarich the R.A.C. sign indicates the way through Glen Dochart to Killin and you just keep going. As you approach Killin you come to the parting of the way; right to Glen Ogle and the south, left to Killin; however, there are a number of things to observe on the way, and the flowers, trees and birds, in particular, will no doubt claim your attention.

Soon after entering the glen you reach Loch Dochart on the left. This loch, in turn, flows into Loch Iubhair (The Loch of the Yew Tree) and from this second loch flows the River Dochart. The ruin on the island in Loch Dochart is said to have sheltered Bruce. The rising ground on the right culminates in the peak of Ben More which is the dominating peak of the district.

A short distance after passing Luib Station you see a by-way at Ledchary crossing the river. This road is an alternative route to Killin, but perhaps it is worth while staying on

9

the road you have followed if only for the view of the Falls of Dochart at the entrance to Killin. The war memorial and the row of cottages near by help to complete a well-balanced picture for the amateur photographer. On the island, in the midst of the falls, is the burial ground of the clan McNab. From time to time pearls have been found in the beds of Scottish rivers, and it has been reported that finds have been made in the River Dochart.

Killin is a lovely district to reach after a day's walking through a bonny glen. The day would be complete with a visit in the evening to Craig Coilliach for the view of Loch Tay and its attendant heights, the dominating one of which is Ben Lawers.

Sixth day.

LOCH TAY AND GLEN OGLE

Route in brief: Killin—Falls of Lochay—Killin—Glen Ogle—Lochearnhead.

Walking distance: 17 miles.

Maps: Ordnance Survey 1″ scale, Nos. 55 and 62.

Before heading south from Killin it is worth while to visit the Falls of Lochay which are a very short distance away in the glen of the same name (a return journey of about seven miles). You could also make good use of a rest day here and enjoy a trip on the loch steamer. Killin, at one time (it must have been a long time ago !), could boast that the Glasgow newspapers arrived at 5 or 6 p.m. *on the same day*, and the same report pointed out that fuel was very expensive. Peat cost three shillings per cartload, and coal the very high price of thirty shillings per ton ! When leaving Killin for Lochearnhead you retrace yesterday's route, but only as far as the Glen Dochart–Glen Ogle road junction. Then, instead of going on into Glen Dochart, you turn up to the left into Glen Ogle. It is a long climb up to the watershed and quite a long descent down to Lochearnhead, but it is a walk you will enjoy all the way. During the first part of the journey look back for parting views of Loch Tay and then, as you approach Lochearnhead, you have an ever-widening picture of Loch Earn and its background of mountains. Superlatives seem to be

much in demand when describing this district, and Doctor
McCulloch uses the word " extraordinary " twice in quick
succession in describing Killin, while a much more recent
writer says that Glen Ogle, " The terrific glen," is " one of
the wildest glens in Scotland." " Wild " better describes
Glen Lochay, but Glen Ogle with its huge and sometimes
fantastic rocks is awesome; there is a quality of alpine
grandeur about it.

The grass-covered road made by General Wade and long
since fallen into disuse, except as a pedestrian track, offers
a pleasing alternative for the way through the glen.

Near the watershed is a lochan named on the map Lairig
Cheile. After passing this fishing pool you enter the glen
proper, the walls of which rise to more than 2,000 feet.

Seventh day.

STRATHYRE

Route in brief : Lochearnhead—Loch Earn—Glen Ample—
Beinn Each—Loch Lubnaig—Kilmahog—Callander—Stirling.

Walking distance : From 14 to 20 miles.

Map : Ordnance Survey 1″ scale, No. 62, or the " Trossachs
Tourist Map."

There are three ways open for to-day's walk. The first is
to follow the road all the way through Strathyre to Callander.
Along this route you come first to Kingshouse where a by-
way branches off to Balquhidder and Loch Voil, the McGregor
country. Then comes a stretch of three miles to bonny
Strathyre, and a little farther on is Loch Lubnaig, a narrow
loch hemmed in by a mighty host of hills, the outstanding
ones being Ben Ledi and Ben Vorlich. Finally, before you
reach Callander, comes the Pass of Leny with its falls and
then, before entering the town, you pass through Kilmahog
where you see the turning for Loch Venachar, where lived the
Wild Horse of Killievronie.

The second route is more strenuous and entails spending
half the day on the hills. From Lochearnhead, follow the
road on the south side of Loch Earn, but only for a very short
distance to Edinample and the Falls of Edinample. Here
you leave the road and follow the stream up Glen Ample.

You have here about seven miles of walking through the heart of the hills to Ardchullarie More on Loch Lubnaig, not far from the eighth milestone from Strathyre. If you wish to add to this walk you can climb the steep eastern slope of the glen to the summit of Beinn Each or the dominant peak Stùc a' Chroin.

The third route, and the best, is the most strenuous and demands at least twenty miles of walking. The route this time is through Glen Vorlich and skirting the Forest of Glen Artney follows the Keltie Water down to Callander. Glen Vorlich is about four miles out from Lochearnhead along the south side of the loch. The path leads up the glen, up into the hills under the shadow of Ben Vorlich and to the head of the Gleann Dubh Choirein where the tracks fork. One leads down the glen to Glen Artney; the other path, the one you follow, goes up the side of a hill stream to a ridge and south-wards on the western side of Meall Odhar and so to the Keltie Water which you follow all the way down to the Bracklinn Falls. From the falls there is a well-worn track into Callander. It is a long, wild, but wonderful walk, and although it includes twelve miles of hard going on the hills it is well worth the effort.

To finish the day, travel by bus or train to Stirling.

Eighth day.

THE OCHIL HILLS

Route in brief: Stirling—Causewayhead—Wallace Monument—Alva Glen—Bencleuch—Tillicoultry.

Walking distance: 10 miles.

Map: Ordnance Survey 1″ scale, No. 67.

The route for to-day, in reverse, is described in the tenth day of The Seventeen Lochs Tour but, nevertheless, there is more to tell to help you make the most of to-day's excursion. Stirling is rightly called the " Gateway to the Highlands," but to obtain this impression the town is better seen from a distance. If you approach downhill, coming from Falkirk, you see in the Castle and its attendant heights, as I have said before, a considerable resemblance to the picture of Salzburg Castle and the nearby mountains.

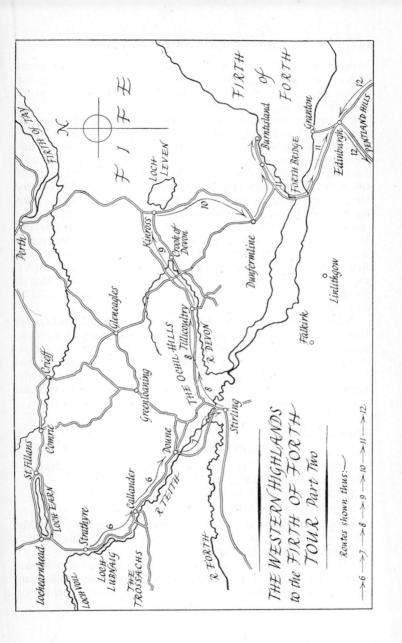

THE WESTERN HIGHLANDS
to the FIRTH OF FORTH
TOUR Part Two

Routes shown thus:—

→6→ →7→ →8→ →9→ →10→ →11→ →12→

From the top of the Wallace Monument, the most completely appropriate of all monuments, you see, as from a watch-tower, the position that Stirling holds and how truly it is the " Gateway to the Highlands."

Go by bus to the entrance to the monument (Tillicoultry or Alva bus) and afterwards walk the short distance to Blairlogie and Logie Kirk. Then go by bus again, along the Hillfoots road, as far as Alva. Here you climb, by way of Jacob's Ladder, into Alva Glen and go on right away to the head of the waters and climb to the watershed. You now bear away to the right, across the boggy lands and peat hags. You have excellent views to the north and then you come to the march fence which leads you to the summit of Bencleuch. If the indicator is in position you can identify the many heights to be seen—that is if you are lucky. This was my first tramping trip after the war and we found only mist on the top. When descending go, at right angles, to the march fence, to the Daiglen, which brings you right down to Tillicoultry.

A longer road to the Hillfoots is to go by way of the Gannel Burn and Maddy Moss and then down the Burn of Sorrow. From the summit of Bencleuch follow the march fence eastwards, keeping to the fence going east (do not follow that branch fence on the right). Then, at the head-waters of the Gannel, cross Maddy Moss. Then comes the downward track *via* the Burn of Sorrow and Castle Gloom to Dollar.

Ninth day.

CROOK OF DEVON

Route in brief : Tillicoultry—Dollar—Rumbling Bridge—Crook of Devon—Kinross.

Walking distance : 15 miles.

Map : Ordnance Survey 1″ scale, No. 67.

This walk provides a great contrast in scenery. In the previous days you have been in the midst of wild hills; to-day you follow meandering by-ways.

From Dollar (bus from Tillicoultry) follow the main Milnathort road, but only for a little more than a mile, when you turn to the right down a small by-way (the second turning on the right out of Dollar) to the River Devon.   Just before reaching the stream, turn to the right and, in spite of little branch roadways, follow in the direction of the stream to the main road at Rumbling Bridge.   Here, from the bridge, you look down into the impressive gorge where the Devon cuts a way through a deep and rocky chasm.   Down below you see the old bridge which once carried the main road over the stream. The Devil's Mill and the Cauldron's Linn must be seen in addition to the view from the bridge.   The River Devon, from source to where it joins the River Forth, runs a course of about thirty miles and descends some 2,000 feet and yet, as the crow flies, the source is only five and a half miles from the mouth.

From Rumbling Bridge, follow the by-way, in line with the river, to come to the Crook of Devon.   Out from the village on the main road to Kinross, follow the first by-way on the right, which, after a long mile, crosses under the railway bridge with Tullibole Castle on the right—a castle built in 1608.   Connected with the castle is the story of a drunken trooper while a ghost is reputed to haunt a pool called the " Trooper's Dubh."   You pass a farmhouse on the road, just past the railway bridge, called " Black Dubh "; perhaps you will get the full story there.

Continue along this road for some four miles and then turn left and, after little more than two miles, you come to Kinross.

All the way from the Crook of Devon you have uninterrupted views of the Cleish Hills.

Tenth day.

CLEISH HILLS

Route in brief : Kinross—Gairney Water—Loch Glow— King's Seat—Knock Hill—The Bents—Craigluscar Hill— Milesmark—Dunfermline.

Walking distance : 14 miles.

Map : Ordnance Survey 1″ scale, No. 67.

From Kinross you go almost due south to Dunfermline, crossing over the Cleish Hills which are not so high as those high and rugged mountains you got to know so well in the earlier part of the holiday. You have wide views though, from the top of these lesser hills, views down the broadening Firth, while across the waters to the south you see the Pentlands.

Your first objective is the little village of Cleish. You retrace your steps, along the road of yesterday, and on a little farther, to the village. Now you are at the foot of the hills and, at once, you follow a path from the village, going south, to the hill road that continues southward. You have the two small sheets of water—Lurg Loch and Dow Loch on your right. Then you have the larger loch—Loch Glow, and you follow a moorland track to the right which ends at King's Seat, a height just about touching the 1,000 feet mark. A path leads you on across Black Rig Moss and Lethans Moss and down to Lethans Farm on the main road. A little way back along the road towards Powmill you turn left and, almost at once, leave the road on the left and climb to the top of the Knock Hill (1,189 feet). Descend to Steelend Farm and follow the farm road south to The Bents. Across the main road continue again south, to Craigluscar Hill (744 feet). You descend to Craigluscar Farm and then continue south along a farm road that runs between two reservoirs that feed Dunfermline; continuing farther south, you come to Milesmark on the main road. You are now on the outskirts of Dunfermline and a little more than a mile of walking will bring you to the centre of the town.

Eleventh day.

THE KINGDOM OF FIFE

Route in brief : Dunfermline—King's Seat—Loch Fitty —Hill of Beath — Monziehall — Aberdour — Burntisland — Edinburgh.

Walking distance : 12 miles.

Map : Ordnance Survey 1″ scale, No. 68.

The Kingdom of Fife seems to be tucked away from the hurry and scurry of the world. On various occasions when rambling in the " Kingdom " I have been impressed by the fact that the villages one passes through appear to be unaffected by the stream of life. On one such excursion, we walked from

Newburgh to Abernethy, by way of Pitcarlie Hill, to descend to Abernethy.

There was quite a crowd of us on this particular visit and one worthy of the village was heard to remark that there had never been so many people there since the " sodgers." It was a very hot day and I think we cleared the village of lemonade and ice-cream. The village of Strathmiglo created the same impression, or, to be more correct, our party created the same sensation. At the end of our day's walk we had some little time to wait for our train and that we spent exploring the village. Judging by the stares and expressions of the people, they wondered what kind of foreigners we were and, even though we had only come from across the Tay, we really felt like foreigners among the people of Fife. However, we enjoyed what their shops had to sell. Another feature of Fife is the peculiarity of the names. There is a farm called Lalathan and others called Clatto Burn and Upper Bunzion. There is a Tor of Kedlock and Dandies' Wood, Kilgourie-knowe, Little Freuchie and Catochill. These names, however, are no more peculiar than some of the queer ones we find on the map of the south of England. What could be stranger than Nether Wallop ?

Leave Dunfermline, by the main road northwards to King-seathill and Townhill, and then go along a by-way for a little under two miles to King's Seat. A little north of King's Seat is Loch Fitty and it is worth the short detour before setting off for the easy climb of the Hill of Beath which is only 785 feet. Descend to the east and join the main road south to Crossgates. Then go eastwards, along the main Kirkcaldy road, for less than a mile, to Fordell, where you turn south along the road that brings you to Aberdour, *via* Monziehall and Old Whitehall. You are now on the Firth of Forth and you follow the shore road going east to Burnt-island. You have an uninterrupted view of the Forth Bridge, which you cross by train to return to Edinburgh, where the tour ends.

You have crossed Scotland from west to east and traversed the rugged and wild scenery of the Central Highlands to come to the more placid county of Fife. You could, of course, spend one of your spare or rest days visiting Crail, farther up the coast, or you could explore the Lomond Hills of Fife. The details of this day's excursion are given in the third day of the Forth and Clyde walking tour. You will have the opportunity of visiting Maspie Den and also Loch Leven. Your difficulty will be not what you should do on the rest days but what to choose from the wide range of possibilities.

Twelfth day.

EDINBURGH AND DISTRICT

You have a choice of town or country excursions on this, the last, day of the tour. For a country walk you should take the first day excursion of the Forth and Clyde tour, the *Route in brief* for which is : Tram to Colinton tram terminus— The Loan—Howden Glen—Glencorse—Loganlee Reservoir —Scald Law—Kirk Road—Penicuik.
Walking distance : 10 miles.
For details, refer to the tour concerned.

If, after reaching Penicuik, you have the time and energy to include another six miles of walking, you should travel by bus or train to Eddleston. If you travel by train, it will be necessary to walk from Penicuik to Pomathorn to catch the connection to Eddleston. At Eddleston Station walk down the station approach to the main road, cross over and follow the track leading uphill to Boreland Farm, from which point a delightful track wanders through the hills to bring you to Portmore Loch, a bonny loch nestling in a fold of the lower slopes of the Moorfoot Hills. At the head of Portmore Loch a footpath bears away to the right. Another track leads ahead to bring you to the road where, by turning to the left, a further mile of walking ends at the main Penicuik road. From here the bus will carry you back to Penicuik and Edinburgh.

If you wish to spend the day in or near Edinburgh, you have much to occupy your attention. One suggestion is first to go to the Castle and visit the War Memorial. Here is the heart and spirit of Scotland.

From the Castle walk the Royal Mile downhill, turning pages of history at every close, to Holyrood Palace. Then climb up to Arthur's Seat and look down on the city.

If you have not had enough, and if there is time to spare, you can see all that Princes Street has to offer. Climb the Scott Monument; listen to the orators at Scotland's Hyde Park Corner, The Mound ; walk in the gardens, see the floral clock, listen to the band, perhaps dance a little, perhaps laze a little.

The Botanic Garden is another place well worth visiting and so, of course, is the Zoo.

VIII

SKYE

AND

THE WESTERN HIGHLANDS

INTRODUCTION

THE combination of walking and train, boat and bus travel makes a most comprehensive tour of Scotland. You begin with an all too brief glimpse of Edinburgh and a peep at its colourful history. Perhaps the most impressive of all the things to be seen in Edinburgh is the floodlit Castle from Princes Street on a black night.

Then on by train to Stirling, the gateway, and to Inverness, the capital, of the Highlands. Beyond that you traverse, still by train, the bleak loneliness of the Highland valleys to come to Kyle of Lochalsh. Then comes the journey to Skye and an all too brief stay on the island. Most likely it will rain but, whatever the weather, the island is worth visiting. You will want to go back many times. After the first week of holiday, you come by steamer through to Mallaig and then, by train and bus, to Onich not far from Glencoe. Mrs. Lamont's at Glenrigh in Onich is a well-known house for trampers.

Finally the tour will end with a memorable sail to Oban, and, if you wish, you can include the trip to Iona and Staffa. Altogether this is a comprehensive and well-balanced tour.

First day.

Travel to Inverness.

In all probability you will travel north on a Saturday and, if so, there are three possible plans from which to choose:

1. Break your journey at Inverness over the week-end.

2. Break your journey at Achnasheen (which is on the route Inverness–Kyle of Lochalsh) for the week-end at Loch Maree.

3. Travel direct to Skye in the one day.

You will travel from Glasgow (Buchanan Street) or Edinburgh (Princes Street) *via* Perth and Aviemore to Inverness, and continue westwards, north of the Caledonian Canal, to Kyle of Lochalsh, where you change to the boat for Portree, Skye. Steamer services are operated by David MacBrayne Ltd., 44 Robertson Street, Glasgow, C.2.

Second day. First plan.

Travel on the local service bus to Daviot and then walk to Culloden battlefield. This is a walk of three or four miles along a pleasant by-way. The return to the city is along the main road, but you have extensive views of the widening Firth and the hills beyond. The excursion need not occupy all the day, and you may, therefore, have time to visit the Ness Gardens and the Castle, from which vantage point you look down on Inverness and the surrounding lands.

An excellent all-day excursion is to travel by service bus to Whitebridge, walk to Fort Augustus and return to Inverness by service bus. This is a good round tour and gives you the complete circuit of Loch Ness. On the outward journey you keep to the loch-side as far as Foyers and then twist and turn through a maze of by-ways to Whitebridge where, during the war, there was a large lumber camp. The walk to Fort Augustus—about ten miles—is through wild and lovely country, impressive in the extreme. In the spring-time the roadside banks in the region of Foyers are carpets of primroses. There is some fine tramping country in the hills and glens on the south side of Loch Ness; some of these old ways are mentioned elsewhere in another tour (see page 208).

Second plan.

ACHNASHEEN AND LOCH MAREE

You can stay at Loch Maree Hotel or at one of the local cottages, and the Sunday can be spent walking along the road by Loch Maree. Here again you will see signs of the lumbermen's activities during the war.

Third plan.

If you have travelled direct to Skye, here is an easy excursion for the Sunday.

KYLEAKIN ROAD AND CARBOST

Proceed up the Tug Road for about a mile, and then turn to the left along the Struan Road. Follow along the road for about three miles, and then keep to the right for Carbost. Here you turn to the right again, to return to Portree.

This walk is not enough for a full day, so it is recommended that you do this excursion in the afternoon, returning in time for the evening meal. Photographers can spend the morning seeking out positions for suitable photographs of Portree Harbour.

There is no steamer service on a Sunday, but it is one of the features of the daily week-day life to see the boat arrive from Kyle.

Third day

Travel to Skye.

If you have stayed in Inverness over the week-end, and I think you will find it worth while, you will spend most of Monday travelling by train and boat to Portree. You traverse wild country in the train and follow in the footsteps of history as you go along the sea-lane to Portree. You have almost as long a journey if you are coming from lovely Loch Maree, because then you have a bus journey in front of you before boarding the train at Achnasheen.

If you are already in Skye, here is to-day's excursion.

Maps : Ordnance Survey 1″ scale, Nos. 24, 34 and 35; ½″ scale, " The Isle of Skye."

Bus to Broadford. Follow the road south-west for one and a half miles, and then proceed along the path on the right of the sharp bend to Coire-chat-achan. Climb north-west to summit of Beinn na Caillich (2,403 feet), walk along the ridge due west to Beinn Dearg Mhòr (2,322 feet), descend west to

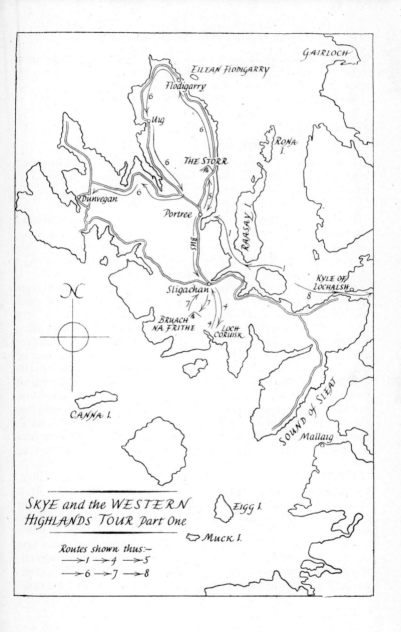

SKYE and the WESTERN
HIGHLANDS TOUR Part One

Routes shown thus:—
→1 →4 →5
→6 →7 →8

the path in Strath Beag. Turn left to Torrin and then turn
right to head of Loch Slapin. Follow the path north through
Strath Mòr to Luib on Loch Ainort. Bus to Portree.

Walking distance : 11 strenuous miles.

Fourth day.

THE CUILLINS' VIEW

Route in brief : Bus to Sligachan—Walk *via* Glen Sligachan
—Dubh Lochans—Druim Hain Ridge—Loch Coruisk—
Return to Sligachan same way.

Walking distance : 18 miles.

If you have good weather this walk gives you a splendid
view of the Cuillins.

You have an early start because the Skye transport bus
leaves at 7.40 a.m. However, you are at Sligachan by 8.15
a.m.—a good time to start the day's excursion.

From the bus terminus, proceed up Glen Sligachan over
the bridge to the left from the hotel, and then follow the path
to the right. You continue for about five miles over a very
rough and wet path to beyond the Dubh Lochans and then
fork to the right at the Cairn. The path now ascends up to,
and over, the Druim Hain Ridge, and it is from the top of
the ridge that, on a day of good visibility, you have the
Cuillins' View. You see Loch Coruisk, Loch na Cuilce and
Loch Scavaig, and the attendant heights, in all their awesome
grandeur. Beyond, and across the stretch of ocean, you see
the Island of Rhum. This is a wild view and a wild walk,
dangerous on a wild day. Read what some of the de-
scriptive writers have to say about the hills of Skye—and take
warning.

Follow along the path to the left from the top of the ridge,
taking care to keep to the cairns until the path ends. It is
from here that you have what is perhaps the finest view-point
for Coruisk. You can, if you wish, make a descent to the
loch from this point.

The return to Sligachan will be back along the route you
came. Bus services for Portree run at infrequent intervals.
If you are a party of six or more it is usual for the bus company to arrange a special car to pick you up at your own time.

GLEN OGLE

Robert M. Adam

W. A. Poucher, F.R.P.S.

KYLEAKIN

THE OLD MAN OF STORR

Fifth day.

THE OLD MAN OF STORR

Evening steamer excursion to Gairloch.

Route in brief : Conveyance to Loch Leathan—Begin ascent by little corrie in left of precipice.

Return to road-way at Loch Leathan—Walk to Portree.

Walking distance : 14 miles.

No visit to Skye would be complete without a visit to the " Old Man of Storr." The scenery in this corner of the island is not so wild and untamed as that seen on the previous day; nevertheless it has the personality of Skye and leaves you with unforgettable memories. There is no bus service on the road you must take, but if you are a small party it will be a simple matter to hire a conveyance from the Skye Transport Company. It will be necessary of course to hire for both the outward and return journey unless you prefer a fairly long road walk after a day on the hill. I do not think you will, but by the time this book is in print there may be a summer bus service on the route.

The conveyance you hire will take you to the base of The Storr at Loch Leathan and, from here, you start your climb. Ascend by the little corrie to the left of the precipice. Your climb will bring you to a vantage point where, from above the cliffs, you have a good view of the " Old Man." From here proceed to the left, along the cliff-edge, and so to the top of The Storr (2,360 feet). Here you lunch and at the same time enjoy the views. Directions for the return are needless. Make your way downhill and back to the loch-side. Then comes the return to Portree, either on foot or by conveyance.

A favourite evening excursion is the steamer trip to Gairloch. If this is operating be sure to join it. The *Loch Nevis* used to do the run before the war, leaving at 5.30 p.m. You had forty-five minutes ashore at Gairloch and arrived back at Portree at 11 p.m. Messrs. MacBrayne state that it is hoped to resume such excursions at an early date.

Sixth day.

REST DAY

Suggested motor excursion to the northern part of island.

You may perhaps think there are too many rest days; and in that case there are innumerable additional excursions to suit your needs. You are recommended, however, not to attempt too much. Most readers will be folk who are confined to the city or town all the year, and whose training for such a holiday is a regular day tramp at the week-end and an occasional week-end excursion. For them, such a tour as is here outlined is quite strenuous enough.

To-day then, relax, and enjoy a round trip by bus or car to the northern end of the island.

If you are a small party you can arrange a conveyance for yourselves with the bus company. Failing that you can join in with another party. The tour, which includes a visit to Dunvegan Castle, covers the following route: The Storr— Loch Leathan—Loch Mealt—Mealt Falls—Kilt Rock— Staffin—Flodigarry—Kilmaluag—Kilmuir—Uig—Skeabost— Edinbain—Dunvegan—Fairy Bridge—Edinbain—Skeabost— Carbost—Portree.

If you visit Dunvegan Castle you will no doubt be shown the Fairy Flag. Legend has it that the flag should be waved three times, but only in dire necessity. Already, according to the story, it has been waved twice.

Seventh day.

THE CORRIE OF THE FLOWERS, ETC.

Route in brief : Bus to Sligachan—Walk *via* Alltdearg Lodge—Corrie of the Flowers (Fionn Choire)—Sgurr à Fionn Choire—Bruach na Frithe—Allt Dearg Mòr—Sligachan— Bus to Portree.

Walking distance : 16 miles.

A record of a hundred years ago says that the prevailing language is the Gaelic, but " the English is gaining ground." It also appears that in those days when one person wished evil to another it was not uncommon to hear it said in Gaelic— " May you never speak properly in English ! "

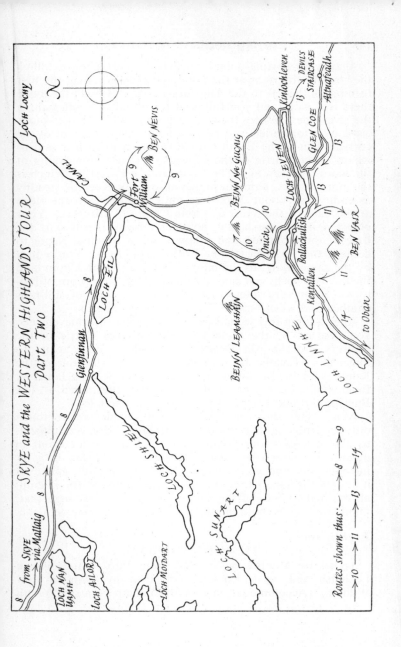

SKYE and the WESTERN HIGHLANDS TOUR
Part Two

LOCH LOCHY

N

LOCH LINNHE

CANAL

from SKYE via Mallaig

LOCH NAN UAMH

LOCH AILORT

LOCH MOIDART

LOCH SHIEL

LOCH SUNART

Glenfinnan

LOCH EIL

BEINN LEAMHAIN

Kentallen

to Oban

BEN VAIR

Ballachulish

Onich

BEINN NA GUCAIG

Fort William

BEN NEVIS

LOCH LEVEN

Kinlochleven

DEVILS STAIRCASE

GLEN COE

Altnafeadh

Routes shown thus:— →8 →9
→10 →11
→13 →14

Again your starting-point is Sligachan. This time you follow the road to the right at the hotel and then go along the first turning on the left to the Alltdearg Lodge. Beyond the lodge there is a path, and you follow it for about two miles along the river-side. Where the stream is joined by a larger burn, cross over to the left and begin a long, gradual ascent of the corrie. This is the Fionn Choire which in English is said to mean, " The Corrie of the Flowers." (Another meaning of the words is given as " The Corrie of the Forest." Which is the more correct, I am not prepared to say.) Keep on steadily ascending for about 2,000 feet until you come to the ridge at the base of the Sgùrr a' Fionn Choire (3,050 feet). Your objective is not the height, however. Instead, you skirt the base of the mountain and follow a series of small ridges to come to the top of Bruach na Frithe (3,143 feet). You return, by the same route, to the base of Sgùrr a' Fionn Choire and then, if you wish, you can add this peak to your score of hill-tops. (It is very interesting to keep a record of hill-tops climbed and when—call it " The Climber's Bag.")

After adding this second peak to your list of achievements, you descend by the same way, through the Corrie of the Flowers and the Allt Dearg Mòr—and so, once again, to Sligachan. Finally, back to Portree, " The Harbour of the King," so named to commemorate the visit of King James V. Incidentally, the old name of Portree is Ceilltarraglen—" The Burying Ground Placed at the Bottom of the Glen."

Note.—This short visit to Skye will enable you to touch only the fringe of its tramping possibilities. It is very difficult to plan a week's tour because it is necessary to leave out so much. However, the excursions just outlined can be your introduction, and you can come back again and again, but it is only the super-strenuous (and super-human) who attempt all the highest hills of the Cuillins in one day—though that, mind you, has been accomplished on more than one occasion.

Eighth day.

TO FORT WILLIAM

Travel by MacBrayne steamer from Portree to Kyle of Lochalsh and on to Mallaig and then by train to Fort William. Accommodation in Fort William or at the Youth

Hostel in Glen Nevis. While in Fort William be sure to find time to visit the West Highland Museum where you will see relics of the '45.

Ninth day.

BEN NEVIS, THE CLOUD-KISSING HILL

Route in brief: Bus to Fort William—Walk to Achintee, following notices to Ben Nevis—Pony track to summit from Achintee—Descend same way if short-cuts not known, to Fort William.

Walking distance: 6 miles and one mountain.

Map: Ordnance Survey 1″ scale, No. 47.

Ben Nevis seems to have grown a little in the last hundred years, because the New Statistical Account published about a century ago gives the height as 4,370 feet. Various meanings have been attached to the name Ben Nevis, but the most appropriate is " The Cloud-Kissing Hill." In fact it is sometimes said that the hill-top is clear about one day a month. Very often, when all other peaks are clear, a cloud will be resting on top of the Ben. There is a route all the way to the top. Follow the notices from Fort William, up the glen pointing the way to the summit. Do not start any rock climbing or work out any short-cuts. There are no half-measures with Ben Nevis. Either you trudge the dreary way along the pony track or you go up with the rock climbers, but only if you are properly equipped.

Ben Nevis attracts those who like to see how quickly they can scale a hill.

The double journey from the town to the summit and back is fifteen miles. In 1903, Ewen McKenzie, observatory roadman, did the distance in 2 hours, 10 minutes. At a later attempt he completed the ascent in 1 hour, 8 minutes.

In 1895 Lieut.-Col. Spencer Acklour did the double journey in 2 hours, 55 minutes. Another record has been set up by two hardy men who climbed Ben Nevis, Snowdon and Scafell in a total climbing time of twenty-four hours !

It seems to be the fashion that when at Fort William you must climb the Ben. That is why I have included it, but to my mind a much more interesting and worth-while climb is

Bidean nam Bian in Glen Coe. In this case you make the ascent from the Clachaig Hotel, but please do not try visiting Ossian's Cave—it is dangerous.

Tenth day.

BEINN NA GUCAIG AND FALLS OF RIGH

Route in brief: Ballachulish Road—First left to summit of Beinn na Gucaig (2,017 feet)—Glen Seilleach—Falls of Righ—Onich.

Walking distance: 10 miles.

Map: Ordnance Survey 1″ scale, No. 47.

This day, being Sunday, does not mark the beginning of your strenuous excursions; these start to-morrow with the climb of Ben Vair. In any case, most likely you had a long journey yesterday, so to-day you can well enjoy introducing yourself to the scenery. The village of Onich spreads itself along the road skirting the loch that leads to the mountains. One can enjoy leaning on the wall, taking plenty of time to stand and stare at the grand sight of the hills. Across the loch you see your objective for to-morrow. Looking up the loch to, and beyond, the narrows you see the sharp summit of the Pap of Glencoe dominating the entrance to the glen. There is ample scope for a camera here, especially at the narrows where there is an excellent view of the loch and the hills nicely balanced with a fringe of trees.

The excursion for to-day need not start until after lunch and there is plenty of time to linger on the way and be back for the evening meal.

You proceed along the Ballachulish road and follow the first turning on the left, which brings you, after a short distance, to the bridge crossing the burn. After crossing the bridge, you start climbing up the hill slope on your left. Your objective is the summit of Beinn na Gucaig (2,017 feet and your route is, by way of a series of easy ridges, to the top. It is not a long and arduous climb, but there is a wonderful panoramic view awaiting you if the visibility is good. You can pick out some of the places you are to visit, and, of course, many spots you will not be visiting. Be sure to have your map with you so as to identify the various heights.

After you have taken your fill of all there is to see, you can spend a little time looking for white heather. If you are there at the right season, you will be sure to find some on this hill-side.

When descending, let your map be your guide to bring you down to Gleann Seilleach, whence you will proceed south, *via* the farm, to come back to the bridge from whence you began the climb. At this bridge there is a clearly defined path to the right, for about five hundred yards, to the Falls of Righ. This is your second objective for the day, so, after that, it only remains to return to the bridge and then back to Onich.

Eleventh day.

TWIN PEAKS OF BEINN A' BHEITHIR (BEN VAIR)

Route in brief : Onich—Ballachulish Ferry—Turn left—First right to station—Climb hill-side to summit (3,362 feet)—Lunch at summit—Ridge walk to Sgòrr Dhonuill—Descent to Gleann a' Chaolais and return to ferry.

Walking distance : 14 miles.

Map : Ordnance Survey 1″ scale, No. 47, or special " Oban " sheet.

If you decide to make this a camping tour be careful to secure your equipment during your absence each day. There are some good secluded places for camping at Onich, but perhaps the safest plan is to obtain permission to camp on private land where your tent and equipment will be watched while you are absent.

This excursion, the first strenuous one from Onich, starts from the other side of the ferry. Walk from Onich to Ballachulish Ferry. Cross over (thank goodness the ferry charge for human beings is less than for a motor-car), turn to the left and then to the right, to the station, and then take, at once, to the hill-side. There is a path from here leading across to and up Gleann a' Chaolais. Then follow the corrie to the left, up the long slope of the hill, to the top of Sgòrr Dhearg where you should have lunch. The summit ridge is narrow and should not be attempted in windy weather. After lunch, follow the ridge to the right and descend about 800 feet to the pass. Start climbing again *via* a fairly easy ridge, to a somewhat dangerous cliff over loose stones and so to the top of Sgòrr Dhonuill (3,284 feet). These two summits are known as the twin peaks of Beinn a' Bheithir. From the top of this second height return by the same route to the pass.

Twelfth day.

REST DAY

Bathing at Kentallen, or climb Ben Alle, or steamer trip to Iona and Staffa, or climb Beinn Leamhain.

You have a number of possibilities before you for the rest day. If you want to make it a real rest day then there is nothing to recommend except complete rest. It would be a good opportunity to write up the diary—a most useful record of the holiday for the future. Do not think, when going over this and other tours, that the daily mileage is light. It is not. Most of the folk reading this book will, it is expected, be keen walkers, but very few will find it desirable to keep up an average of more than twelve to fifteen miles per day for two weeks, and, even then, it is very desirable to have at least one rest day each week. If you want to be on the move, you have the option of two hills across the Corran narrows at Ardgour, Beinn Leamhain or Ben Alle.

To attempt the climb of one of these heights, both of which give good views of the Firth, involves about ten miles of walking—not too strenuous. If you are keen on bathing you can make the trip to Kentallen Bay, which involves crossing Ballachulish Ferry and following the road from there.

A really strenuous day, if you want to attempt another mountain, is to climb Bidean nam Bian in Glen Coe. Do not forget, however, that this undertaking means a seventeen-mile walk and the ascent of one of the highest hills in the district. The slopes are steep in parts, but if you keep away from the screes and cliffs you will not get into any difficulties. Start the ascent from near Clachaig Inn.

It is possible to do the steamer trip to Iona and back in the day from Kentallen Pier. It means an early start and it is for you to decide whether it is worth it. According to the present time-table you can do this tour on Thursdays only in the summer season. You change boats at Oban.

If you are keen to do this excursion it might be as well to cut out the rest day and so leave for Oban a day ahead of this itinerary, thus giving you a clear day at Oban for the trip.

Thirteenth day.
THE DEVIL'S STAIRCASE

Route in brief : Bus from Onich to Kinlochleven. Walk *via* pipe-track to Valve House—General Wade's Road from Valve House—Devil's Staircase—Altnafeadh—Glen Coe—Loch Triochatan—Ballachulish Ferry—Onich.

Walking distance : 16 miles.

Map : Ordnance Survey, 1″ scale, No. 54.

The Kinlochleven bus service operates from Ballachulish Ferry and, according to the current time-table, there is a departure at 9.35 a.m. There is also a service from Fort William *via* Onich calling at Onich post office at 9.50 a.m.

On the return you may be looking for a bus to cut out the long road walk back to the ferry. A study of the time-table, however, is not very encouraging because the few buses going your way do not seem to fit in with your times. (Check up on this when at Onich.)

Kinlochleven, at the head of the loch of that name, is hemmed in by high hills, and the only apparent escape ahead is over those hills. That is the way you will go to-day, up and over and down to Glen Coe, and its new road.

From the bus terminus, proceed to the left and then across and up the pipe-track to the Valve House 1,000 feet up. From this point you cross the hills by the old military road marked on the map as " General Wade's Road." These roads have long since ceased to be used except as tracks for folks like us wanting to cross the hills, and in consequence traces are fast disappearing. That is the case in this instance, and so you may have difficulty in finding your way. It is quite indistinct in parts, also the route winds quite a lot before the summit is reached. It is about four miles to the top but the climb is well worth while if only for the impressive view obtained of Glen Coe. The scene is aptly described by H. V. Morton who says of this district:

" Imagine the best of Switzerland and the Rhine valley mixed up and poured out across Scotland in a broad wild belt of beauty."

From the summit you descend by way of the Devil's Staircase to the glen at Alltnafeadh. Here is a good place for lunch. Then take to the road—the new road—down Glen Coé past Loch Triochatan to Clachaig where you will be glad to have tea—lashings of it. After that you have the long road walk back to the ferry.

Fourteenth day.

TO OBAN

Route in brief: Onich—Ballachulish Ferry—Kentallen—Boat to Oban.

Walking distance : Not more than 10 miles.

Map : Ordnance Survey 1″ scale, " Oban District."

Consult the MacBrayne steamer time-table. At present the Friday steamer leaves Kentallen in the early afternoon. Check times, however, with the up-to-date time-table. This does not give much time for an excursion, so a good plan is to leave from Onich about 10 a.m. and take a packed lunch, then, upon arrival at Kentallen, picnic by the loch-side and spend a lazy time until the steamer comes. You are due to arrive at Oban about 4 p.m. so, after tea, you will have the opportunity to do a little exploring. An evening walk across the golf course is very pleasant. Beyond the golf course, follow the road under the railway bridge, by the loch, to Glen Cruitten. Then, where the road bears to the left, there is a footpath that cuts off the bend in the road. When rejoining the road, turn to the right, to Loch Nell and beyond, where you will come to the main road. Or, if you wish, return by the footpath, which leaves the road at Loch Nell and skirts the little hill of Cnoc Mòr, to bring you back to the golf course.

Oban is one of the few places in Scotland where shinty is popular. I remember watching the local team playing Kyle Athletic in the semi-final of the Shinty Cup. The game is like hockey but without the restrictions. You can swing the stick as much as you like, hit your man where you like, but

I am not sure whether you are allowed to bite your opponent. At half-time the supporters support the players with whisky. (That was in pre-war days.)

Fifteenth day.

Return home by train or bus. The route by rail or road is through the Pass of Brander and Glen Lochy to Crianlarich and then through Glen Dochart and bonny Strathyre to Stirling and the south.

IX

THE DEE AND THE DON

INTRODUCTION

THE Don valley is not so well known as that of the Dee, but the scenery it has to offer is a fitting introduction to the wider variety that awaits you along the valley of the Dee. Starting at Aberdeen, you traverse much of the Don valley by train (or bus) and then start walking at the quiet town of Alford. From there you meander through the pleasant vale of Alford and the bosky den of Kildrummy. From now on you follow the Don to its source and, before crossing the hills to Deeside, you make a detour through Glen Avon to Scotland's highest town—Tomintoul. (Some say Leadhills holds that distinction.) Once on Deeside you have much to claim your attention. It is not intended that you shall go right to the source of the Dee, but you will be very near it when you walk to the entrance of the Lairig Ghru. To continue right on to the Pools of Dee and return in one day is too long an excursion. You will like the clachan of Inverey with its monument to a native man who held, with distinction, a high post with the King of Bavaria. It is unique that the inscription is in Gaelic, English and German. From the Linn of Dee you follow the stream all the way to the sea. Through Braemar and the broad lands of Invercauld and on to Balmoral, Ballater, Aboyne and Banchory—all beautiful places. Sometimes your walk is by the banks of the river or along a nearby road and at other times you climb the heights and look down on the stream as it winds a course between the hills, through forest and pasture—and so to the sea at Aberdeen.

A wonderful winter holiday can be spent at Ballater and upper Deeside. Living there for two winters has convinced me of that. All January and February the snow was on the ground continuously. The milkman delivered each day by sledge and the heavy luggage cart was mounted on a sledge. Snow walks on the nearby hills and the valley roads were a joy and so were skating and tobogganing. There was a certain amount of ski-ing, but no organised winter sports. The rosy-tinted top of Lochnagar made a winter's morning picture from Ballater to be remembered always.

First day.

Travel by train or bus to Aberdeen from Glasgow or Edinburgh.

Second day.

THE VALE OF ALFORD AND THE DEN OF KILDRUMMY

Route in brief: Aberdeen—Alford—Bridge of Alford—Toll of Mossat—Kildrummy Castle—Den of Kildrummy.

Walking distance : 10 miles.

Map : Ordnance Survey 1″ scale, No. 44.

Travel by train or bus from Aberdeen to Alford in the Don valley. The best of the valley starts at Alford and you are not missing anything by covering the first stage by train or bus.

Alford is a quiet country town, obviously the centre of a farming community. Most of the town is lined along the main street, at the head of which the road divides, and you take the right-hand way. There are no rugged mountains here, instead you have a sweet, smiling valley with rounded, wooded hills sheltering the pasture lands from the northland storms. Yet in winter these roads fill up with snow and conditions become arctic. It has not been an uncommon experience for travellers to be snowed up for a week-end at Bridge of Alford.

Not very far out from Alford you come to the cross-roads. Here you turn to the right for the Bridge of Alford, not more than half a mile distant. You turn to the left here, cross the bridge and follow the line of the Don for some miles until you come to the Toll of Mossat. Immediately before the

Toll you pass the Bank House on your right. At the Toll of Mossat you turn to the left and follow the winding road as far as Kildrummy Hotel which is your destination for the night. Here there is excellent accommodation, summer or winter. It is amazing how severe the winters can be here. Heavy snow-ploughs are needed, especially on the section of road up from the Toll of Mossat to Kildrummy Hotel. The bread-van sometimes follows the plough and people from outlying farms wait at the road-end for their overdue supplies.

After your evening meal continue up the road to walk through the Den of Kildrummy and, when returning the same way, be sure to visit the ruined castle of Kildrummy, which stands in the midst of well-tended grounds.

Third day.

GLEN KINDIE AND CORGARFF

Route in brief : Kildrummy—Mill of Kildrummy—Towie—Glen Kindie—Don Valley—Corgarff.

Walking distance : 10 miles.

Map : Ordnance Survey 1″ scale, No. 44.

When you leave the hotel turn to the left, as if going back to the Toll of Mossat, but follow the first turning on the right past the sawmill and the duck-pond. In a short time you come to the compact community of houses clustered round a telephone call-box.

The smiddy and the meal mill are the twin centres of activity here. You have a choice. Either you stand and watch the blacksmith and gaze with awe on a field of derelict vehicles and farming implements or you can inspect the meal mill and discuss almost any type of business with the miller—pigs, hens, cycles, petrol and so on. It is all in the day's work. Nearby was a Dominion lumber camp during the war.

Go on along the road past the Mill of Kildrummy, up the hill alongside the fringe of trees and then, near the top of the rise, turn to the right along a half-hidden by-way which takes you across a windswept upland and down to the Don again. At the foot of the road you turn to the right to come to Towie, where vehicles have considerable difficulty in

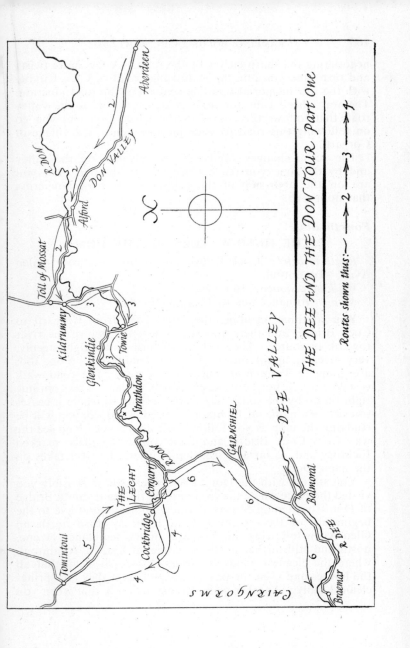

THE DEE AND THE DON TOUR Part One

Routes shown thus:— → 2 → 3 → 4

negotiating the sharp curves of the road. A few more twists
and turns and you join the main valley road of Glen Kindie,
with the war memorial standing sentinel at the road junction.
The way ahead calls for little guidance. This is the valley
road that follows the course of the River Don and you go
on following this road to your journey's end—the village of
Corgarff.

The scene changes subtly as you advance up the valley
and by the time you reach Corgarff you discover that you
are on the door-step of the wilds. To-morrow you cross
that door-step.

Fourth day.
THE HEAD-WATERS OF THE DON

Route in brief: Cock Bridge—Inchmore—Inchrory—Glen
Avon—Tomintoul.

Walking distance : 16 miles.

Map : Ordnance Survey 1″ scale, No. 44.

You continue on along the valley road from Corgarff to
Cock Bridge, and there you still follow the line of the river
towards its source. The road proper turns to the right steeply,
very steeply, uphill on the way to Tomintoul. You, too,
are going to Tomintoul, but not this way. The road walk
is wild enough but your way is much wilder. You continue
right on up by the south side of the stream, to where it ceases
to exist as a name, at Inchmore. Needless to say you will be
studying the map as you follow these directions. You see the
way from Cock Bridge and then comes the place marked
Inchrory and, as far as I see, that is where the river takes on
the name Don.

You started with the Don at Aberdeen, where possibly you
visited the place where the river entered the sea (tram to Bridge
of Don from Union Street) and now you say good-bye to the
beginnings of the stream and, at Inchrory, turn north up
Glen Avon following the footpath, or the semblance of one,
north and still farther north, to come, at last, to Tomintoul,
where the cleanest winds of Britain blow—so clean that all
the houses and even the pavements look as if they are spring-
cleaned daily. Another claim to distinction is that when you

W. A. Poucher, F.R.P.S.

SLIOCH AND LOCH MAREE (*see page* 141)

call for a whisky you are asked if you want " proof " or not. One farmhouse I know in these parts could produce a bottle " over proof," but such a drink has to be treated with great respect—otherwise it takes your breath away.

There is an interesting route through the hills joining Glen Avon with Nethybridge. This road joins the road crossing the plateau a little north of Nethybridge. The route is referred to in the eleventh day of the " Cairngorm Tour."

There is a youth hostel at Tomintoul, as well as boarding-houses and hotels.

Fifth day.

OVER THE LECHT

Route in brief : Tomintoul road through and over the hills, *via* The Lecht—Cock Bridge.

Walking distance : 10 miles.

Map : Ordnance Survey 1″ scale, No. 44.

During the early part of the eighteenth century General Wade was responsible for the building of many roads, and, in consequence, wherever you go in the Highlands you find frequent references on the map to a " military road." You traverse one of these roads for part of your walking distance to-day. You are returning to Cock Bridge and Corgarff, whence you came yesterday, but this time by The Lecht military road.

From the head of the town street of Tomintoul, turn to the left and, very shortly, gain the main road, where you turn to the right and face the long road to the Well of the Lecht. The road seems to bore into the hills and the nearer you come to the glen-head the more you wonder how the road can escape from such a wilderness. It does, however, by making an unexpected right-hand turn and you find yourself in a barren and forbidding glen with walls sloping up to the 2,000-feet contour level. About one and a half miles short of this sharp turn—the Well of the Lecht—is the farm of Blairnamarrow, where a track begins, going across the hills to the River Don above Cock Bridge.

From the Well of the Lecht to the head of The Lecht is about three miles and the road ascends in that distance from

400 feet to 2,500 feet. There is a gate across the road at this contour point and from here the road switchbacks to the Hill of Allargue and then descends like a corkscrew to Cock Bridge. While on the heights you have a very extensive view over one of Britain's wildest regions.

Near the Well of the Lecht are old ironstone workings, the ore from which was carried in creels to the furnaces at Nethybridge. According to an account of the period, " the enterprise was more remarkable for boldness than wisdom . . . the most profuse and profligate set that ever were heard of in this country. Their extravagances ruined themselves and corrupted others. They used to display their vanity by bonfires of tar barrels and opening hogsheads of brandy to the country people by which fire some of them died in one night."

Sixth day.

THE GAIRNSHIEL

Route in brief : Glas-choile—Gairnshiel—Hill Road to Balmoral Castle—Braemar.
Walking distance : 10 miles.
Map : Ordnance Survey 1″ scale, No. 44.

The road from the north which you traversed yesterday is wild and the way you take to-day, southward, is just as wild, but ends on a tamer note in Deeside.

You say good-bye and mount the road through Glas-choile. From Cock Bridge, follow the main highway eastwards until you see the turning to the right, through Glas-choile, over to Gairnshiel. This road is very rough in parts. *Hints to Climbers in the Cairngorms*, dated 1890, advises, for ease in walking, that gentlemen should remove collars and cuffs, and ladies should " kilt their skirts."

At the watershed a track branches away to the right across to the lower part of Gairnshiel, but you keep to the road down the steep rough way to Gairnshiel where a " steeple " bridge of the steepest variety spans the river. Hereabouts, if you know where to look, are black currants free for the picking. These bushes continue to flourish untended in the overgrown gardens of ruined houses.

At the junction of the road with Glen Gairn, turn to the right, and cross the hills by a route every bit as stony as the one you have just left. By the time you have reached the highest point on the way you feel as if you are on the roof of the foothills of the Cairngorms. The better view is ahead as you descend to Deeside, a fitting introduction to the river you are about to explore. As you descend to Balmoral and Crathie you have an uninterrupted view of the Lochnagar massif.

At Crathie Church travel by bus to Braemar passing *en route* the forest of Ballochbuie on the left and the extensive Forestry Commission plantings on the right.

Seventh day.

REST DAY

You have now had five days of continuous walking, and to-morrow you have a strenuous day ahead, so make good use of this day and relax. Little more need be said for this lazy day, but if you wish for a picnic excursion, carry out the suggestion given for the Braemar rest day in the " Grampians' Tour."

A further suggestion is that, in the evening, you walk to Inverey, obtain lodgings and be ready to move off from there the next morning for the long walk to the head-waters of the Dee. This will reduce the next day's excursion to twenty-one miles and also enable you to travel with the minimum of kit.

Eighth day.

THE HEAD-WATERS OF THE DEE

Route in brief : Auchindryne—Linn of Corriemulzie—Linn of Dee—Glen Lui—Derry Lodge—Devil's Point—Glen Dee— Chest of Dee—White Bridge—Linn of Dee—Inverey.

Walking distance : 21 miles as from Inverey.

Maps : Ordnance Survey 1″ scale, Nos. 43 and 49, or the special " Cairngorms " map.

You have been to the beginning of the River Don and now comes the visit to the head-waters of the Dee, the source

of which is at the Pools of Dee, high up in the pass through
the hills, just at the commencement of the sternest part of
the walk through the Lairig Ghru. It is not intended, however, to go as far as this to-day, otherwise your mileage would
be too heavy. A round trip of not less than twenty-one miles
is strenuous enough for one day.

Every bit of the way is full of interest. The first five miles
take you along the road to Inverey. At one time this road led
through woodlands almost all the way and, perhaps, forty
years from now there will once more be trees there. At
present it is mostly wreckage of trees. This was one of the
contributions of Deeside to the war effort, and for part of
these war years Canadians thronged this, and other parts of
Deeside, felling, shipping and milling.

A stretch of road near Corriemulzie has been spared and
so, for all too short a distance, the road is fringed with tall,
straight, stately pines. The russet carpet of pine needles
fringing the road, the mossy banks, the twilight of the woodland vistas, combine to make a picture one can keep in
memory for the dark days of winter.

At the Linn of Corriemulzie you must spare the time to
scramble down and explore this titbit in an area crammed
with loveliness. Then on to Inverey and beyond to the Linn
of Dee. The highway finishes, but you keep on and into the
high hills. Just beyond the bridge over the Linn, turn to
the right (the gate you see immediately on your left marks the
way to the Geldie Burn and Glen Feshie). Follow the road a
little farther and you see another gate on your left. This is
your way up Glen Lui to Derry Lodge. A new gate has been
erected to bar the way, but this does not affect pedestrians.
You now follow the route as if you were going through the
Lairig Ghru. Consult your map and you will see the way
marked. Beyond Derry Lodge the track swings away to the
left to come to the River Dee in Glen Dee, below the Devil's
Point. This is as far as you go to-day, so turn your back on
The Cairngorms and return, along the banks of the Dee, to
what is called the Chest of Dee and White Bridge, at the
junction with the Glen Feshie track. So you come back
again to the Linn of Dee and finish up for the night at
Inverey.

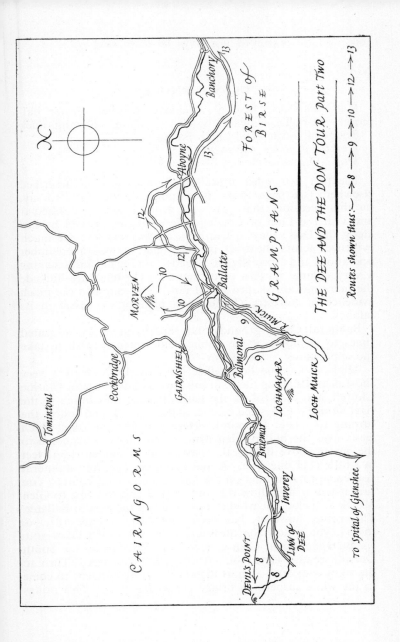

THE DEE AND THE DON TOUR Part Two

Routes shown thus :- →8 →9 →10 →12 →13

N

Tomintoul

CAIRNGORMS

Cockbridge

GAIRNSHIEL

DEVILS POINT

LINN of DEE

Inverey

Braemar

Balmoral

LOCHNAGAR

LOCH MUICK

TO Spital of Glenshee

GRAMPIANS

MORVEN

Ballater

R. MUICK

Aboyne

Banchory

FOREST of BIRSE

8

8

9

9

10

10

12

12

12

13

13

Ninth day.

GLEN GIRNOCK

Route in brief : Inverey—Braemar—Crathie—Easter Balmoral—Bovaglie—Glen Girnock—Littlemill—Strathgirnock—Bridge of Gairn—Old Line—Ballater.
Walking distance : 15 miles.
Map : Ordnance Survey 1″ scale, No. 44.

The first five miles of walking is over ground described elsewhere (see page 164). It is sufficient, therefore, to say, on this occasion, that you walk from Inverey to Braemar and visit the Linn of Corriemulzie *en route.* Travel by bus along the Dee valley to Crathie; on the way you see much evidence, across the river on the right, of war-time lumber operations and especially the " roads " on the hill-sides making a very definite pattern of extraction. On one bare hill-side the markings are shaped like a fan. You can also see much evidence of Forestry Commission planting—a forest in its infancy.

Balmoral Castle grounds and gardens are open at stated times to members of the public, and you may wish to take the opportunity to visit them.

Alight at Crathie Post Office from the bus. Walk a very short distance along the road towards Ballater, to visit Crathie Church, and then follow the path opposite the church to the river bridge. Cross the bridge, and the road, and follow the turning to Easter Balmoral. Here you find the road which leads over the hill to Glen Muick; go this way to come to the moors above Balmoral. This ascent is sudden, 1,361 feet in a little over one mile. About two miles out from Balmoral you come to a turning on the left which is your route. You can, if you wish, follow the route ahead and so come to Glen Muick at Inchnabobart and then go down the glen to Ballater. This route, however, has been described on page 187, so, to-day, you follow the turning on the left which takes you, *via* Bovaglie, down Glen Girnock to Littlemill on the South Deeside road. Here you are in Strath Girnock. Turn to the right and, after a short distance, turn to the left, to come to the white suspension bridge across the river. This brings

you to Bridge of Gairn on the North Deeside road, whence
you walk along the riverside path called the " Old Line " to
Ballater.

Tenth day.

GLEN GAIRN AND MORVEN

Route in brief : Ballater—Old Line—Bridge of Gairn—
Glen Gairn—Hill of Candacraig—Morven—The Nameless
Glen—Tullich—Pass of Ballater—Ballater.
Walking distance : 13 miles.
Map : Ordnance Survey 1″ scale, No. 44.

You cover familiar ground at the beginning of the day's
walk. Go by way of the " Old Line " to the Bridge of Gairn,
and then follow the main road back towards Ballater until
you come to the first turning on the left along the east bank
of the glen. There is also a road along the west bank of the
river—a road that branches off the main highway on the Braemar side of the Bridge of Gairn. The east-side road is lined
for part of the way with hazel trees, and in season there is a
plentiful supply of nuts.

Continue along this winding switchback road as far as you
can go and, when you come under the shadow of the Hill of
Candacraig, remember to go up the road to the right. At
the top of the hill, instead of going to Morven Lodge, bear
to the right, along the path across the face of Morven. The
path is indistinct in parts, but if you persevere, you will come
at last to the beginning of the Nameless Glen which leads
to the main North Deeside road at Tullich.

There is also another interesting track across the slopes of
Morven, starting near the top of the road, by Morven Lodge.
This path goes through the Forest of Bunnsach to Boltinstone
where a road takes you, *via* Logie Coldstone, to the A.A.
box on the North Deeside road at Cambus o' May, a few miles
east of Ballater.

The Nameless Glen lies between Culblean Hill on the east
(the scene of a battle in 1325) and Crannach Hill on the west.
Tullich Glen is the next-door neighbour to the west and when
you reach the main road you are at the mouth of Glen Tullich,

almost opposite the ruined church of Tullich. Turn east-wards, along the Ballater road, and you face a perfectly balanced picture of the town framed in high hills.

Where the road forks, go by the right-hand way along the Pass of Ballater and, when in the centre of the pass, turn to the left along what appears to be a private drive. When you come to the gate of the big house follow the path on the left across to Ballater.

Eleventh day.

REST DAY

You will find Ballater an excellent place for a lazy day. Refer first to the " Grampians' Tour " and you will find recommendations what to do with your rest day. If the old lumber camp of Glen Muick still stands, you will find it of great interest; it is, or was, just off the road on the way to the Pannanich. The huts of this camp were built by Newfoundland lumbermen and are similar to the log cabins of their own country. After the Newfoundlanders left, the camp was used for housing Italian prisoners who were working on the land.

If you wish to carry out an excursion instead of resting, you can do one of the excursions mentioned in the " Grampians' Tour," *e.g.* eighth day—The Water of Tanar ; ninth day—Birkhall and Dalliefour ; tenth day—The Coyles of Muick.

An easy walk for an evening is across the golf course and *via* the " Old Line " to the Bridge of Gairn, returning by way of the Pass of Ballater to the Aberdeen road, near the Tullich Churchyard and along the road to Ballater. The " Old Line " is the original railway track built beyond Ballater towards Braemar—a project which was abandoned.

The Churchyard of Tullich contains the graves of three Newfoundlanders, two of whom died as the result of an accident near their camp. About a mile farther along this road on the way to Cambus o' May is a bobbin mill where birchwood is used to make pirns or bobbins.

Another short excursion, especially for the evening, is the climb of Craigandarroch, which rises from the streets of Ballater. Yet another is to walk up to the Pannanich and then follow one of the woodland paths to Cambus o' May Bridge. From here you take the main road to Ballater.

Twelfth day.

DINNET MOOR

Route in brief : Ballater—Cambus o' May—Dinnet Moor —Loch Davan—Milton of Logie—Wester Coull—Scar Hill— Braeroddach Loch—Craig Ferrar—Aboyne.

Walking distance : 10 miles.

Map : Ordnance Survey 1″ scale, No. 44.

Travel by the Aberdeen North Deeside bus to the A.A. box at Cambus o' May, at which point you begin walking along the branch road to the left. In August the early heather (bell heather) on the Moor of Dinnet is a sight unequalled anywhere, for the whole moor is one huge bright purple carpet. If you first saw a true picture in colour of the moor you would say that it was fantastic and that reality could not be like that. It *is* like that, it *is* fantastic and it *is* real.

You are on the way to Loch Davan and *en route* you have Loch Kinord on your right and, at one point, on the left, you pass the Vat Burn with its mad jumble of rocks known as The Vat. Then you come to the building which housed the water-clock. Upon a recent visit of mine the clock was not working, but perhaps its activities will have been restored when you go that way. A little beyond this house you turn to the right, skirting Loch Davan. This road is fringed in part with cherry trees. Then you come to the cross-roads at Milton of Logie. Go straight ahead along the road which is laid across a bog. When walking along this stretch of road you become aware of the unevenness of the road caused by the unstable and boggy foundations. Two miles out from Milton of Logie turn to the right to Wester Coull and go, by a pathway across country, to the main road near Aboyne. Your route takes you to Scar Hill (984 feet) where you have a view over the surrounding country; then on to the small Braeroddach Loch and finally by Craig Ferrar to the Aboyne road, whence a further two miles brings you to the town and the end of the day.

Thirteenth day.

THE FOREST OF BIRSE AND GLEN CAT

Route in brief : Aboyne—Dee Bridge—South Deeside Road—Birsemore—Burn of Cattie—Glen Cat—Feughside—Banchory.

Walking distance : 17 miles.

Map : Ordnance Survey 1″ scale, Nos. 44 and 45.

The town of Aboyne is situated on the north side of the river and, for to-day's walk, you must cross the Aboyne Bridge over the Dee and turn east along the South Deeside road in the direction of Banchory. You have the choice of two routes. The first begins at Birsemore, which you come to almost at once after turning east from Aboyne Bridge. Follow up the turning at Birsemore and, after about a mile, and a little before reaching the farm of Drumneachie, go by the footpath on the right across the hill to the head of Glen Cat. The alternative route is by the South Deeside bus from Aboyne Bridge to Marywell on the service from Ballater to Aberdeen.

For the second route, which starts at Marywell, follow the turning which you find a short distance along the road to the right. This is the way up Glen Cat, a distance of three miles to the road-end where you join the footpath mentioned in the first route.

You now continue by a footpath across the hill—and not up the glen—to Bullachan at the head of the road in Glen Feugh. The footpath—the Fungle Road—continues more or less south to join The Fir Mounth track four miles from Tarff-side and then on through the hills to Glen Esk and Edzell. That is off the route for this tour so you go by the road all the way down by the Water of Feugh to Banchory. A few miles down the road you come to Feughside Inn and from here it would be useful to continue by bus to Banchory. Be sure to alight at the Bridge of Feugh before entering Banchory and see the Falls of Feugh.

Fourteenth day.

TO ABERDEEN

There are a number of interesting excursions in the neighbouring countryside of Banchory, but the wildness of upper

Deeside is lacking and the remainder of Deeside, from Banchory to Aberdeen, can be seen quite well from the South Deeside bus. You have done plenty of walking in the two weeks and to-day can well be spent in Aberdeen. It is suggested, therefore, that you travel by bus in the morning to Aberdeen and then, in the afternoon, go down by the Fish Market and watch the River Dee flow into the North Sea. Compare the river with the mountain burn you saw up at the Lairig Ghru and with the swirling waters in the Linn of Dee. While you are in Aberdeen you may wish to visit the kippering houses and also watch the girls gutting the herring for the kippering.

Afterwards travel, by tram, from Union Street to the Bridge of Don, where you see the river merging with the ocean. In this case you will think of the wild day west of Cock Bridge when you turned north from the head-waters and struck through Glen Avon to Tomintoul.

A study of the map and a knowledge of the district show a number of interesting walks if you wish to linger in the Banchory neighbourhood. You can explore Glen Dye or climb Clochnaben or you could walk to the summit of the Slug Road and descend along a by-road back to the Dee valley. You have, however, seen the best of the two valleys and have done well. You went by bus through the Don valley to Alford, instead of walking, and the best advice now for the end of the tour is to finish your walking at Banchory and go by bus to Aberdeen.

When in Aberdeen be sure to visit the biggest hole in Scotland—the granite quarry at Rubislaw. A tram will take you from Union Street and the conductor will tell you where to alight. It is a sight you will never forget. It looks as if all the granite in the world must have come out of that hole.

X

THE GRAMPIANS AND
THE MOUNTH TRACKS

INTRODUCTION

THIS is a wild, mountainous region and one to be treated with every respect, especially if this is your first introduction to the Highlands of Scotland.

The district to be visited covers a wide area to the east of the Cairngorms. Perhaps it could be said that the road from the Spittal of Glenshee *via* the Devil's Elbow to Braemar, is the division of the two ranges while the valley of the Dee forms the northern boundary. In the east the hills rise in easy contours from the coastal plain.

The road up Glen Clova leads you to the heart of things; from then on the way is through and over much of the Grampians and you traverse the old rights-of-way known as the Mounth Tracks. These roads have known the print of wandering feet far back in history and cross the Grampians at various points. The most easterly track across the hills is known as The Slug, now a motor-road connecting Stonehaven with Deeside, near Banchory. Another motor-road following the line of an old track is the Cairn o' Mount from Feughside to Fettercairn. The other routes crossing the mountains are now derelict roadways, fast merging with the heath and heather, or just simple footpaths which, in places, too, are disintegrating and becoming increasingly difficult to follow. The Cairngorm Club *Journals* contain interesting reports of rights-of-way cases affecting the Glen Tanar Mounth Tracks and the Tolmounth or " Jock's Road " which connects Glen Clova with the Cairnwell. The Scottish Mountaineering Club Guide, *The Cairngorms*, makes good reading before and after this tour; there is much of interest regarding the Mounth Tracks on page 39.

During the war years many lumbermen of Canada and Newfoundland came to live and work in Scotland. Their camps were to be found in many remote places, such as the slopes of Glen Clova, the Linn of Dee and the Forest of Birse, and many interesting stories are told of their arduous work.

First day.

To Kirriemuir.

Travel by train to Forfar and change to the local train for Kirriemuir; or by train to Perth, and thence by bus to Kirriemuir.

Coming from the south you will travel from Glasgow on the Aberdeen train and change at Forfar junction for the short run on the local line to Kirriemuir, the terminus.

Kirriemuir, the birthplace of Sir J. M. Barrie, is a small country town of twisted by-ways and narrow streets, with queer-sounding names, and is little changed from the days when Barrie wrote of the place under the name of Thrums. The street scenes were changed during the war when Polish Forces were billeted there and the Newfoundland lumbermen worked in the woods out Cortachy way. There is a plaque on the wall of the school, placed there by the Poles in grateful recognition of the kindness and hospitality shown them. The Newfoundlanders, too, have left behind them a happy memory of big-heartedness and generosity, and when they returned home they took with them some of the local girls as wives and with them carried something of the spirit of Scotland.

The white-washed Airlie Arms will surely remember the Newfoundlanders and perhaps best of all their foreman, Billy Greening, who at one time was a drive boss and a trapper. It was not easy to get him to talk, but when he did he could tell some grand tales of trapping in the winter and of the river drives to the mills when the spring thaws set the rivers moving again. By the way, the Airlie Arms is a good place at which to stay.

Kirriemuir (Kirrie for short) is surrounded by fruit gardens and when you leave the town, on the second day of the tour, you will pass many fields of raspberries.

Second day.

GLEN CLOVA

Route in brief : Kirriemuir—Cortachy—Dykehead—Right- or left-side road through Glen Clova—Millton of Clova.

Walking distance : 15 miles.

Maps : Ordnance Survey 1" scale, Nos. 50 and 58.

From the town square of Kirriemuir follow up the narrow street called The Roods, and straight on up the hill, where the road bears to the right, to come to cross-roads. Here you turn to the left and then, at Cauldhame Wood, which is on your left, turn right, and downhill, to the bridge over the Prosen Burn. The road climbs uphill, skirting the policies of Cortachy Castle, and then, at the top of the hill, it forks. To the right it leads to Cortachy; the left fork, however, is your way on to Dykehead, where again there is a dividing of the ways. The road to the left leads up Glen Prosen, and it is a dead-end, although there is a track over the hill from the village of Prosen *via* the Hill of Drumwhern, down to South Inch Downie in Glen Clova. Your direct route, however, is not to go up Glen Prosen but straight ahead up Glen Clova.

You have now something like ten miles of walking up the glen to your destination at Millton of Clova, but it is a good road for walking as there is little traffic on it.

Across to the left, on the top of the wooded Hill of Tulloch, you see the Airlie Memorial Tower, and across to the right are the hill-sides of Benscravie where the timber was cut during the war by the Dominion lumbermen.

North of Tulloch Hill is a peculiarly named hill—The Goal.

The district seems to specialise in unusual place-names. There is the Hill of Badhappies and Marywee Hill and the Tops of Fieshill.

At last you come to Millton of Clova, your destination for the night. There is accommodation at the youth hostel, or perhaps at one of the cottages, but it is advisable to book up for the hostel in advance. There is no way through the

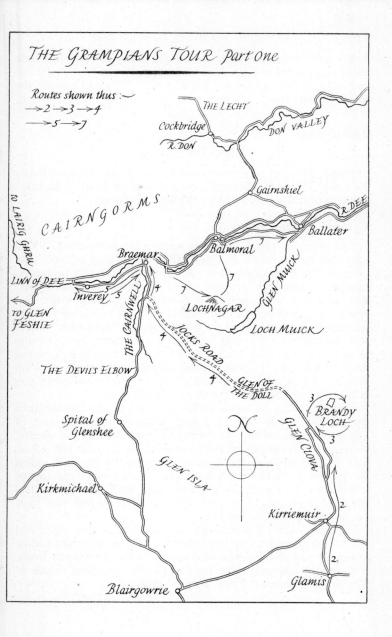

THE GRAMPIANS TOUR Part one

Routes shown thus :—
→2 →3 →4
→5 →7

THE LECHT

Cockbridge

R. DON

DON VALLEY

Gairnshiel

R. DEE

CAIRNGORMS

Ballater

to LAIRIG GHRU

Braemar

Balmoral

GLEN MUICK

LINN OF DEE

Inverey 5

THE CAIRNWELL

4

7

7

LOCHNAGAR

LOCH MUICK

TO GLEN FESHIE

JOCKS ROAD

4

4

GLEN OF THE DOLL

3

BRANDY LOCH

3

THE DEVIL'S ELBOW

GLEN CLOVA

N

Spital of Glenshee

GLEN ISLA

Kirkmichael

Kirriemuir

2

2

Blairgowrie

Glamis

valley for vehicular traffic, although plans have been made for a road from the head of Glen Muick. In fact, the road was actually started before the war but, for some reason, the work ceased almost at once.

Third day.

BRANDY LOCH

Route in brief : Corrie Burn—Corrie of Clova—Benty Roads (2,753 feet)—Brandy Loch—Craigs of Loch Wharral— Loch Wharral—Ben Tirran—Millton of Clova.

Walking distance : 8–10 miles.

Map : Ordnance Survey 1″ scale, No. 50.

The mileage given above is somewhat misleading. You may not do as much as eight miles of walking or you may do more than ten miles, but each mile you do will be heavy, except on the high ground where the way may be firmer. This is a day when you will, more or less, make your own route. Right from the doorstep of Millton of Clova you are on the hill-side and there are no recognised footpaths. There will be sheep-tracks, and perhaps a rabbit-run used by the shepherd as his daily track. Get out your map and trace the route proposed. Having shown yourself what there is to do you can be on your way, and decide as you go whether you would like to add another hill or exclude one.

From Millton of Clova follow the line of the Corrie Burn up the hill. This stream comes down from the Corrie of Clova. As you ascend, bear to the left, away from the stream, so as to reach the end of the Corrie Rocks on your left. You will ascend beyond the corrie, to come to the hill called Benty Roads (2,753 feet), a peculiar name, from the top of which you have quite an extensive and wild view. You feel that although this is your second day of tramping you have come very quickly to the hills.

Descend back to the corrie, but this time to the other end of the crags, and so to Loch Brandy. Then you will follow along the top of the crags, looking down on the Brandy Loch, but do not lose elevation by descending the steep slopes of The Snub between the two lines of crags.

DEE VALLEY AND LOCHNAGAR

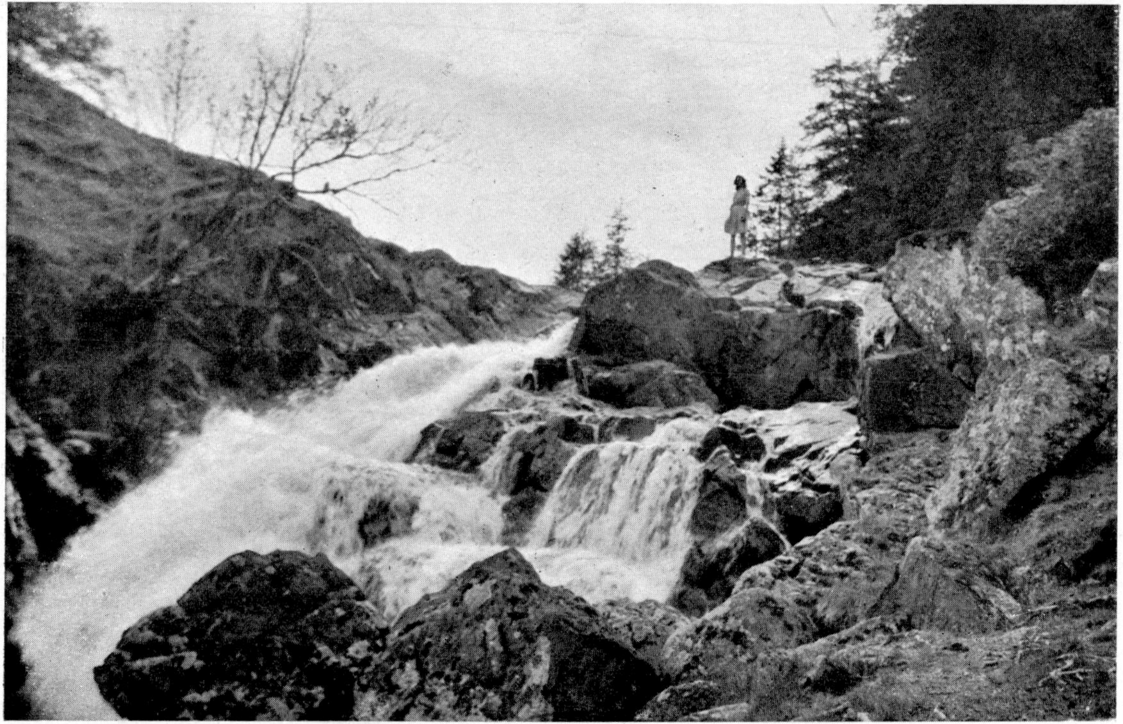

Tom S. Hall

Skirt round the front of Green Hill, keeping at about the 2,600-feet level, and so you will come to the Craigs of Loch Wharral where, again, you look down on a loch. Beyond the Craigs you have a short and fairly stiff climb to the top of Ben Tirran (2,860 feet). You descend to the loch and then follow the stream which flows out of it, down to Millton of Clova.

Fourth day.

JOCK'S ROAD

Route in brief : Millton of Clova—Road to the head of Glen Clova—Glen Doll—Tolmounth—Jock's Road—Glen Callater—Cairnwell Road—Braemar.
Walking distance : 25 miles.
Maps : Ordnance Survey 1″ scale, Nos. 44 and 50.

The road through Glen Clova continues for about four more miles, through a valley like a deep cut in the high hills. At Braedownie the road proper finishes and three different routes start. Two of the routes march together, going to the right to Moulzie, following the line of the River South Esk. At Moulzie the track divides. One route goes over Capel Mounth to the head of Glen Muick, and the other goes right to the head-waters of the River South Esk, to Bachnagairn, and then to the west, *via* Sandy Hillock, to the steep face of Glen Muick.

Your route is to the left, a little past Braedownie, following the White Water in Glen Doll. On both sides you are hemmed in by high walls and, at the far end, you climb out and cross through the hills. It is wild, just how wild you cannot realise until you are there ! The highest point on your route is 3,014 feet, and that is a little before you cross the Tolmounth to descend, steeply and quickly, to Glen Callater.

The wildest part of the walk is the section of open hill-country between the head of Glen Doll and Glen Callater, and this is a distance of five or six miles. This is Jock's Road, a right-of-way about which there has been litigation, but it is still a right-of-way. From the head of the glen you have about eight or nine miles of walking, down past Loch Callater, to the Cairnwell road, where, by turning to the right, you have a short road walk of a little over two miles to bring you to Braemar.

Jock's Road crosses the hills over what is called the peat-moss of Fafernie and is an ill-defined track, in fact in parts you discern the way by means of sticks at intervals. It is not safe to undertake this walk except in good weather.

Fifth day.

LINN OF DEE

Route in brief : Braemar—Linn of Corriemulzie—Inverey —Linn of Dee—Return to Braemar.

Walking distance : 13 miles.

Maps : Ordnance Survey 1″ scale, Nos. 43 and 49.

You can make this into a long day by doing the excursion right up to the Devil's Point, by way of Derry Lodge, and coming back by way of Glen Dee to the Linn of Dee. Further details will be found in " The Don and the Dee " tour.

The road walk from Braemar to the Linn of Dee and back makes a very comfortable day. You linger at the Linn of Corriemulzie and, perhaps, picnic in the main street of Inverey. This main street consists of a sleepy by-way lined on one side with cottages standing somewhat aloof in their own flower-decked gardens. The other side of the road is flanked by a strip of grass which in turn is sheltered by a belt of trees.

To many trampers the name of Inverey brings back the memory of Maggie Gruar and her elastic house. It is said that no matter how full up her house may have been she had always room for another—that is if the traveller was carrying a rucksack.

On the strip of grass which lines the street of this Highland clachan is a monument with the inscription in three languages —Gaelic, English and German. The memorial is for one John Lamont of Corriemulzie, " whose name is written in the history of science as Johann von Lamont, Astronomer Royal of Bavaria."

The Linn of Dee might more properly be called " The Pot of Dee." The waters surge through a narrow channel of rock, and ages of the swirling and boiling has worn the rocks into circular pots. You will see on the rocks the marks of the old wooden bridge, and also you will see a small memorial stone which warns you that it is dangerous to go too near the edge. This small memorial stone is to commemorate the death by drowning of Gwynn and Katie in 1927.

Just near the Linn of Dee is a former Canadian lumber camp. The place was also used by other military bodies but, later, was left empty. There are excellent kitchens, good bunk-houses, a theatre and water is laid on.

Sixth day.

REST DAY

There is a bus service which runs over the Cairnwell to the Spittal of Glenshee and this might be an interesting day-excursion from Braemar for your rest day. Bus times can be obtained in Braemar.

In the village, just a few yards up the Cairnwell road, is the house where R. L. Stevenson lived at the time when he wrote *Treasure Island*. The house is on the left-hand side of the road and there is a stone tablet, suitably inscribed, above the door.

A very enjoyable picnic day can be spent by walking a few miles up the Cairnwell road and picnicking by the side of the stream. Then, after lazing as long as you feel inclined, cross the bridge over the stream and return to Braemar along the road on the other side of the valley skirting the golf course.

Seventh day.

LOCHNAGAR

Route in brief: Braemar—Danzig Bridge—Ballochbuie Forest—Blackshiel Burn—Meall Coire na Saobhaidhe—Cac Càrn Beag (3,786 feet, summit of Lochnagar)—Summit Rocks —Red Spout—Jacob's Ladder—Gelder Shiel—Crathie.

Walking distance—One mountain.

Maps : Ordnance Survey 1″ scale, Nos. 44 and 50.

Of all the excursions in the Dee valley and the nearby hills the memory of Lochnagar stands out as the grandest of all.

These were winter excursions, and on the day when we " first-footed " the mountain, indeed, we proved that nothing could surpass such a winter's day. It was bitterly cold, the deep snow hard and crisp and the sun blazing down. On the summit of Lochnagar it was not wise to take our gloves off—at least for long—otherwise there was the danger of frost-bite. Although we climbed in winter, the route we took was the same as for the summer. The walk starts at the Danzig Bridge, a white foot-bridge over the Dee near Invercauld House. We motored from Ballater (Station Garage is good for hiring) to the bridge, but the distance to Braemar is not too far. In any case, you should be able to make use of the service bus.

The bridge leads you across to Ballochbuie Forest and to the Danzig Shiel where you follow a forest road bearing to the left. After a short distance you leave the road and strike uphill, through the forest to the open country. You should now find yourself in the wide glen through which flows the Blackshiel Burn; follow up the course of the burn, and then leave the stream and ascend, as you go forward in line with the water. You are now on the slopes of Meall Coire na Saobhaidhe. We lunched at a huge boulder which marks the bare hill-side and acts as a guide. From here the gradient is steep, but this boulder-strewn slope is the last lap ere the summit is reached. We found a summit coated smooth with ice and had to dig down to find the mountain indicator.

From the summit, follow the ridge round to the far end of the precipices, and then descend by Jacob's Ladder. From the foot of The Ladder make a bee-line across the open hill-side for the Gelder Shiel whence a road leads all the way to Crathie.

Travel from Crathie to Ballater by service bus or hired car.

This is an all too short account of such a wonderful excursion. There is not space enough to tell of the summit views, the loch called Lochnagar, which is collected in a fearsome bowl of the mountains, or of watching the distant herds of deer. Lochnagar is indeed the best of the holiday, better than Jock's Road or the majesty of the head-waters of the Dee.

Eighth day.

THE INVISIBLE ROAD

Route in brief : Ballater—Glen Muick Bridge—Ballintober
—Mount Keen and Brechin Mounth Track—Pollagach Burn
—Pannanich Hill—Craig Coillich—Ballater.

Walking distance : 10 miles.

Map : Ordnance Survey 1″ scale, No. 44.

From Ballater, cross the bridge to the south side of the
river and turn to the right to Glen Muick. A short distance,
perhaps a mile, brings you to the Muick Bridge, but, in the
meantime, you have pleasing views of the river as it curves
round the carse laid out as a golf course. You see the dark
woods of Dalliefour, on the left of the river, and then, as a
background to the scene, you have the skyline known as the
Coyles of Muick. This minor range acts as an outrider for
the more important and mightier range of Lochnagar, which
you would see if you had a higher elevation.

At the Muick Bridge is the parting of the ways. Ahead is
the Glen Muick road; to the right is the way to Birkhall,
and to the left your way—the Mounth track over the hills
and far away. At this road-junction is a tablet commemorating
an occasion when Queen Victoria reviewed troops prior to
their sailing for South Africa.

The Mounth road leads to the keeper's house and beyond,
through the woods, to the open hill-side. This is more than
a path. At one time it was a reasonably good road, but now
it is engaged in a losing battle with the elements and nature
generally. It is ideal, however, for walking—a road across a
wilderness of barren hills. The way ascends always, and
curves round the shoulder of the hill, to bring you to the
watershed and a mountain pool. The road dips a little now,
and comes to a wooden footbridge, and then vanishes. It
has vanished but, if you will look to the summit of the rising
ground, you will see a signpost that has outlived the road.
Make for that signpost, and you will find the way marked
with sticks. When you reach the signpost at the fence you
see that it points the way to Brechin and to Ballater. This
signpost has the distinction of being one of a select band
which remained in position all through the war. In the

direction of Brechin you see Mount Keen, and between you and the mountain is dark Glen Tanar.

The Mounth track you are on curves downhill to the Water of Tanar whence you could continue downhill, in line with the stream, down the glen to the South Deeside road and Ballater. A more interesting way, however, is to turn to the left at the signpost and follow the march fence until you come to a line of shooting-butts bearing across the hills to the left. Go, in line with these butts, across the valley, up the other side, and then, as straight as you know how, to the hill of Craig Coillich above Ballater. Then descend through the remains of the woodlands, felled during the war, to Ballater Bridge.

An exhilarating walk at any time of the year.

Ninth day.

BIRKHALL AND DALLIEFOUR

Route in brief : Ballater—Muick Bridge—Birkhall—Dallie-four—Gairn Bridge—The " Old Line "—Ballater.

Walking distance : 10 miles.

Map : Ordnance Survey 1″ scale, No. 44.

This is a day when you are never very far from Ballater, but you follow some very interesting by-ways and woodland paths. Much of the district is now operated by the Forestry Commission, and you will see trees in various stages of development from the nursery upwards.

Cross the Ballater Bridge to the south side of the Dee and turn to the right to Glen Muick. At the Muick Bridge turn neither to right nor left, but go straight ahead up the glen. The road meanders, corkscrew-fashion, on its way to the hills but, after about two miles, you see the semblance of a road at Brockdhu where you branch off to the right, downhill, past the school, and on to the road at the Mill of Sterin on the other side of the river. Very soon you will come to the Forestry Commission office and nursery. Next door is the house of Birkhall, a residence on the royal estate. Beyond Birkhall you are not long in coming back to the Muick Bridge, but you turn off at the forester's house, about a quarter of a mile this side of the bridge. Here you see a roadway on

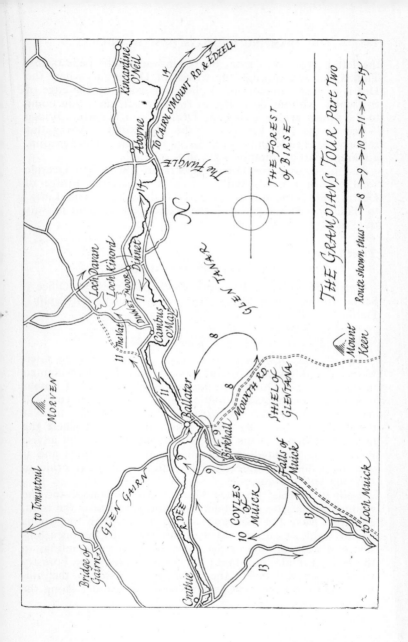

THE GRAMPIANS TOUR Part Two

Route shown thus : → 8 → 9 → 10 → 11 → 13 → 14

the left barred by a gate, but giving access to pedestrians. This is the way through the woods of Dalliefour, where the Dee is a close companion. Follow this track on the edge of the wood, without deviating to right or left, until you come to the Gairn bridge across the Dee. It is a big white bridge —one of the type peculiar to the Dee valley. Along this route you will see indications of natural forest regeneration, apparently an uncommon sight in Scotland.

Having crossed the Dee, you come to the North Deeside road. Turn towards Ballater, and then, at the Bridge of Gairn, follow the path on the right along the " Old Line " to Ballater. This survival of the abandoned Braemar railway track is now a bosky path close to the Dee.

Tenth day.

THE COYLES OF MUICK

Route in brief : Ballater—Birkhall—Forestry Office—School-house—Glen Muick—Coyles of Muick—Littlemill—Dalliefour—Ballater.

Walking distance : 12 miles.

Map : Ordnance Survey 1″ scale, No. 44.

The Coyles of Muick is a range of hills between Glen Muick and Balmoral. Much of the hill-side has been planted in recent years. During the war years a great deal of timber was felled in Deeside, but planting continued, as you will see, up Glen Muick. The forester, Mr. A. Munro, lives at the house, on the Glen Muick road, at the point where the by-road branches to the right for Dalliefour. He will advise you how to avoid doing damage to the plantations and if you are sufficiently interested he will take a great pride in showing you the nurseries.

Follow the road up Glen Muick, past the school and the white wooden gate, and, later, the iron gate across the road, and then leave the road and wander up through the woods on the right. Continue through the woods to the open hill-side and walk up one of the Rides between the plantings to the high ground. No doubt, as the trees grow, the Forestry Commission will define the tracks to be used to the hill-tops. Once on the high grounds you can wander along the ridges and enjoy the views of hill and valley. Then, when it is necessary to descend, go northward, after you have picked out the by-way which leads down to Littlemill, through Glen Girnock. Turn right at Littlemill along the South Deeside road to come to Ballater.

Eleventh day.

THE BURN OF VAT

Route in brief : Ballater—Cambus o' May—Vat Burn—The Vat—Loch Kinord—The Water Clock—Loch Davan—Dinnet—Ballater.
Walking distance : 11 miles.
Map : Ordnance Survey 1" scale, No. 44.

The North Deeside road out of Ballater brings you, after almost three miles of walking, to the Bobbin Mill near Cambus o' May. Almost opposite is the old right-of-way, at one time a built road, across the slopes of Culblean Hill, to Loch Davan. Follow this road for about two miles, and then go downhill, taking the Vat Burn as your guide. This is only a short stream, and brings you to a huge pot in the rocks caused by the action of the waters. This pot is called The Vat. You should approach it from the lower side and creep through the gaps in the rocks into the cauldron. From The Vat it is about 400 yards downstream to the road. Here turn to the right, and follow a gravelly track a few yards farther on to the left. This takes you by the waterside of Loch Kinord after which you turn to the left, back to the road at the water clock. Here you turn to the right and, skirting Loch Davan, turn to the right again, to come to the main North Deeside road at Dinnet and the bus back to Ballater.

Twelfth day.

REST DAY

Ballater is an excellent place in which to spend a rest day. I could spend more than a day there doing nothing in particular, talking with this person or that. But then I know Ballater and the folk. If you are interested in fishing you will

surely talk with Smith, the saddler, or if photography is your
hobby then go and see Jimmy Reid at his wooden shop at
the corner of Station Square. His pictures of Lochnagar are
excellent.

This is a rest day, so relax. Stroll around the golf course—
it does not matter in the least whether or not you play golf;
the course has a bonny situation, and if you walk the eighteen
holes you will see the surrounding country from various
angles and always it is pleasing. The River Dee makes a
wide sweep round the low lands on the outskirts of Ballater
and, in so doing, forms a boundary for the course. The now
bare slopes of the Pannanich Hill are a reminder of the activity
of the war years when heavily laden trucks rumbled to the
sawmill or to the waiting waggons at the station.

The local dances were quite an event in Ballater, especially
during the earlier days of the war.

That is your rest day. There are really no excursions you
could do because you will be seeing all the places at some
time during the tour.

An easy walk would be to do the round of the Pass of
Ballater and see the old churchyard and ruin of Tullich Church,
where the Scots dance, " The Reel of Tullich," is said to have
been composed and danced for the first time.

Thirteenth day.

LOCH MUICK

Route in brief: Braemar—Crathie—Balmoral—Hill Road
—Loch Muick—The Glen—Falls of Muick—Birkhall—
Ballater.

Walking distance : 12 miles.

Map : Ordnance Survey 1″ scale, No. 44.

Travel by bus to Crathie and alight at the church, the
foundation-stone of which was laid by Queen Victoria in 1893.
She presented the communion plate of silver and most of the
stained glass. King George V and Queen Mary gave the
communion table of Iona marble as a memorial to Edward
VII, and in 1911 they presented the three-centuries-old screen
of carved oak. The pulpit contains nineteen different varieties
of Scots granite.

Opposite the church is a path that leads to a bridge over the river to the South Deeside road, where a by-way leads uphill to Balmoral village. Here is a road which takes you over the hill and down to Glen Muick, near to Loch Muick. Turn to the right when reaching the glen road and continue to the beginning of the loch.

You now have three possible routes. You can continue up the loch-side as far as you like and return the same way, or return at once down the glen to Ballater, using the road on either side of the river according to your fancy. On the way down you come to the Linn of Muick—a fine place for your picnic.

Fourteenth day.

CAIRN O' MOUNT

Route in brief : Ballater—South Deeside bus to the Bridge of Dye—Glen Dye—Spittalburn—Cairn o' Mount—Clattering Bridge—Craigmaston—Fettercairn—The Gannachy—Edzell.

Walking distance : 20 miles.

Maps : Ordnance Survey 1″ scale, Nos. 45 and 51.

Travel by Strachan's South Deeside bus to the turning for the Cairn o' Mount road, about five miles west of Banchory. The bus stops at the hotel where the road comes over from Kincardine O'Neil. Your road crosses the Water of Feugh, bears away to the left, climbs through the woodlands, drops down to a water-splash, and then takes you along Glen Dye down to the bridge at Spittalburn. From here you climb still higher, leaving the woodlands behind, to come to bare moors where snow-poles line the road. For a long period in winter this road is snow-bound. So to the summit of Cairn o' Mount, with its wide-spreading view to the coast, and then downhill, quickly and steeply, to Clattering Bridge. You are back again in cultivated lands and in four miles you reach the village of Fettercairn with its triumphal arch and its village cross. You will like this village, but not the arch.

Another stretch of road walking brings you *via* Gannachy Water, to Edzell—the end of the tour. Be sure to look over the bridge at The Gannachy—it is a bonny sight.

You have done 20 miles of walking to-day but you will agree that it is a fitting end to such a fortnight of tramping in the Grampians.

Finally go by bus to Brechin, where there is a train connection for the south.

Spelling Note.—Spital and Spittal are both correct. Accordingly the name is Spittal in the text, and Spital in the map.

XI

THE CAIRNGORMS

INTRODUCTION

HERE is an itinerary fit for heroes, and do not under-estimate just how strenuous this tour can be. You start off with a very long and arduous excursion right through the hills, the wildest and highest range in Scotland, and you must be prepared for such a trip. Be sure you are physically fit to undertake the distance involved and to endure the conditions prevailing in the district. Do not go alone, and be careful in choosing your companions and to satisfy yourself that your clothes and kit are suitable. Be sure you take all that is needed but do not carry a rucksack as big as a mountain-side. The golden rule is, " cut to a minimum and divide by half."

After the first long day of tramping you are given a week of normal excursions in which to explore the fringes and foot-hills of the Cairngorms. The Cairngorms are a household word to all trampers, but there are many little places, gems in the general setting, that often escape notice. Loch Vaa and Loch Alvie have been included in the itinerary, and the former is particularly lovely, perhaps because of the sudden-ness with which one comes upon it. Then come the wind-swept by-ways around Carrbridge, and the lonely Dava Moor, with mile after mile of bog and by-way. The sleepy, half-forgotten tracks between the Tomintoul road and Nethybridge give you the impression that these by-ways lead to the homes of the fairies. Then, as a grand finale, comes the Lairig Ghru. It really is a man-sized walk, but if you select a long June day of good weather you should go through without undue fatigue. You will obtain a great deal of pleasure in advance if you read what others have to say of this most famous of passes. H. V. Morton tells of his well-nigh super-human effort of doing the Lairig Ghru and then through the hills again to the Blair Atholl road. Then there is the grim experience told in *Travels of Tramp Royal*, by Matt Marshall. The Scottish Mountaineering Club *Guide to the Cairngorms* is also a mine of information.

A three-day alternative called a " Commando Tour " is included to cover the tenth, eleventh and twelfth days. This alternative is stiff and you must be really tough to do it. It will, however, give you an unforgettable experience and will enable you to realise just how wild and awesome this high range of mountains can be.

First day.

Travel, by train, from Glasgow or Edinburgh to Aberdeen, and continue the same day to Ballater, by train or bus. There are two bus services to Ballater—Strachan's and Alexander's. The latter follows the north Deeside route and the former the south side.

Stay overnight at Ballater. There is a wide range of accommodation: youth hostel, boarding-houses and hotels.

Second day.

Travel by bus to Braemar from Station Square, Ballater. Break the journey at Crathie, if desired, and visit Crathie Church and Balmoral. The grounds of Balmoral Castle are open to the public on certain days of the week. An uninter-rupted view of the Castle is obtained from a short distance up the Gairnshiel road out from Crathie. A few miles beyond Crathie, and shortly before coming to Invercauld House gates, you see Ballochbuie Forest on your left across the river and new plantations of the Forestry Commission on the right. Then, when crossing the Dee at Invercauld, you see the old bridge on the left, and next, over the water and across the fields, you see Invercauld House and, finally, just before entering Braemar, you pass the old Braemar Castle.

You have an easy day of walking to-day, but there are sterner days ahead. From Braemar you have only five miles of walking ahead of you to come to Inverey and the object

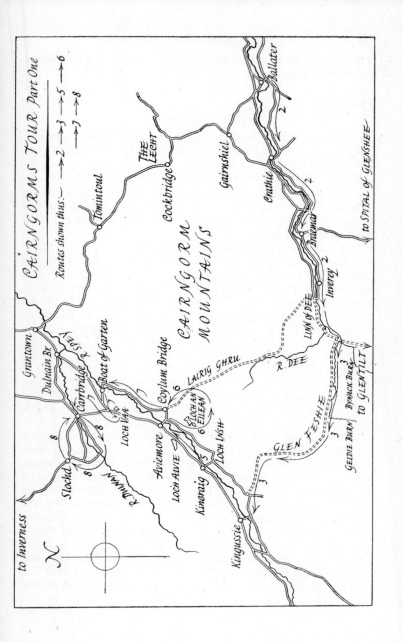

of doing this short distance is to cut down the heavy mileage
for the next day.

Third day.

GLEN FESHIE

Route in brief : Inverey—Linn of Dee—Geldie Burn—
Geldie Lodge—River Feshie—Tromie Bridge—Kingussie.
Walking distance : 26 miles.
Maps : Ordnance Survey 1″ scale, Nos. 43 and 49.

A road-way leads into the hills from both ends of the
walk and the in-between part, through the wildest of hill
scenery, is connected by a rough track. The highest point on
the way is 1,834 feet.

The Linn of Dee is the beginning (or the end) of three
important routes through the Cairngorms. There is the
Lairig Ghru route *via* Derry Lodge, and then the Glen Feshie
and Glen Tilt tracks, which march together for a short distance
from the Linn of Dee. In fact an alternative route to the
Lairig Ghru goes with the Glens Feshie and Tilt routes as
far as White Bridge. Here the alternative Lairig Ghru route
turns off at Glen Dee and the route you take for Glen Feshie
continues in the direction of the Bynack Lodge. You see
the beginning of your road immediately across the bridge at
the Linn of Dee where a gate, across the left-hand turning,
bars the route for vehicular traffic.

The Glen Tilt track continues right on to Bynack Lodge
and beyond, to come out eventually at Blair Atholl.

Your way branches off to the right, a little before Bynack
Lodge, and follows up the side of the Geldie Burn, and leads
to the head-waters of the burn. From the Geldie ford you
have about three miles to the River Feshie which eventually
leads down to the plain. The first contact with the Feshie
is where you join another track which continues up, by the
side of the river, and then loses itself in the hill. Soon after
joining the river and the path you come to the River Eidart
and another footpath which follows part of the way up
Eidart Glen. From the point where you first join the glen,
near its beginning in the hills, you have about six miles of
walking down to the road, turning to the left at Achlean.

A TIMBER OPERATION ON THE FRINGE OF THE MOORS

W. A. Poucher, F.R.P.S.

GLEN FESHIE

Straight on is the route to Loch Insh and Kincraig, but you turn left at Tromie Bridge for Kingussie and the end of your long walk.

Fourth day.

REST DAY

After the strenuous excursion of the previous day no doubt you will want to take things easy to-day; but there are a number of gentle excursions from which to choose if you feel you want to do something.

Loch Gynack is only two miles away and the old Ruthven barracks a mere stone's-throw distant, while the nearby Creag Bheag (1,593 feet) is a magnificent vantage point from which to view the Cairngorms. A Cairngorms' panorama card is obtainable in the local shops at a very modest price.

Loch Alvie is a few miles south of Aviemore, on the main road, near Lyn Wilg Hotel, where a tree grows by the road-side, the roots of which are a very queer shape. The tree itself, for some unknown reason, is known as " The Limp Earwig."

A by-way leading into the hills from the main road at Easter Lyn Wilg, about a mile out to the south of Aviemore, leads you to the River Dulnan. Check this with your map and, if you so desire, you could evolve quite an interesting excursion.

Fifth day.

LOCH INSH

Route in brief: Kingussie—Ruthven—Tromie Bridge— Loch Insh—Kincraig—Loch Alvie—Aviemore.

Walking distance: 16 miles.

Map: Ordnance Survey 1″ scale, No. 43, or special map, " Cairngorms."

Leave Kingussie by the road at the station to Ruthven, where you turn to the left to Tromie Bridge. You were here previously on your way from Glen Feshie but now you turn left, to the north. You are in line with the main road across the valley, but it is much better on this quieter route, and, after passing through Insh you have the opportunity of seeing

Loch Insh. Where the road skirts its far side you have an excellent view of the loch where the foreground is dominated by a green knoll crowned with a small church. After the road has traversed the low ground you cross the River Spey and ascend, steeply, through the small village of Kincraig, to the main road. If you wish you could turn off the main road at Milehouse to Feshiebridge and so continue all the way to Aviemore on this side of the river. However, it is better to go to the main road and turn to the right to Aviemore. By following the main road you pass Loch Alvie—another loch where a church helps to complete a scene of peaceful beauty. Most of the way along the roads to-day you are on nodding terms with the Cairngorms. On the third day you did a strenuous stretch of twenty-six miles but, if that is a record for you, a Cairngorm record is much more ambitious. In 1908 a group of five men climbed six of the highest Cairngorm peaks in nineteen and a half hours. Then in 1932, the same route was covered in sixteen and a quarter hours by Mr. W. D. Hutcheon and two others, of Turriff.

From Loch Alvie, and Lyn Wilg Hotel, you have a further two miles to your journey's end at Aviemore.

Sixth day.

LOCH AN EILEIN

Route in brief : Aviemore—Inverdruie—Polchar—Loch an Eilein—Loch Gamhna—Inverdruie—Aviemore.

Walking distance : 11 miles.

Map : Ordnance Survey 1″ special map, " Cairngorms."

The road out of Aviemore, in the direction of Coylum Bridge, should become quite familiar to you. This is the route for the Lairig Ghru and also for the walk to Carrbridge. To-day you go only a short distance along this road. The approach from Aviemore makes a fitting introduction to this day, which is to be spent in the Rothiemurchus Forest. First you cross the Spey and follow a road recently fringed with stately trees. Woodlands stretch over a wide area and much timber was cut by the Canadians and the Newfoundlanders for war needs. Timber for earlier wars has also been supplied from Rothiemurchus. An old report states: " The woods formerly occupied an area of about sixteen square miles; and during the many years of the great war with France . . . they became disastrously thinned and are only now in the course of revival."

After leaving the old avenue behind, you come to the cross-roads at Inverdruie. Continue ahead, and then follow the road-way that curves away to your right. You are soon in the woodlands and a short distance only brings you to Loch an Eilein. The woodland track carries you to, and encircles, the loch in which there is a small island, and on that island there is a ruined castle said to have been a stronghold of the Wolf of Badenoch.

At the far end of the loch the track continues to another and smaller loch—Loch Gamhna—and then swings round and back to the side of Loch an Eilein and eventually to the road you left. Here you have a choice of two roads home. You came by the road on your left, so I suggest that you return by the other road *via* Polchar to Inverdruie and Aviemore.

There is an interesting chart on sale in Aviemore for a few pence indicating the peaks seen from Aviemore station.

Seventh day.

AVIEMORE TO CARRBRIDGE

Route in brief : Aviemore—Coylum Bridge--Loch Pityoul-ish—Grantown-on-Spey—Kinveachy—Loch Vaa—A.A. box —Deisher—Carrbridge.

Walking distance : 17 miles.

Maps : Ordnance Survey 1″ scale, Nos. 43 and 38.

It would be simple to follow the main road all the way from Aviemore to Carrbridge, but the more interesting way is to follow the road given in brief above. On this route, between Aviemore and the A.A. box, were three lumber camps during the war operated by Canadians and Newfoundlanders.

Go by the road to Coylum Bridge, passing on the way the left-hand turning for The Dell, a farmhouse hotel. At the Coylum Bridge cross-roads, turn to the left along the valley road, which brings you to the small but entirely delightful Loch Pityoulish. Across the valley you see the hills of Kin-veachy, now almost completely devoid of trees. Linger as your fancy pleases by the loch and then continue to Boat of Garten.

As you enter the village, after crossing the river bridge and going under the railway bridge, turn to the left. Then, at the village centre, where you have the station on your left, you turn right and almost at once turn left. And now you are on a by-way which brings you out at Kinveachy on the main Aviemore–Carrbridge road. Turn to the left along the main road but, after a few hundred yards, and before reaching the railway bridge, you traverse a footpath on the left through the bushes to Loch Vaa. The scene awaiting you is unexpectedly beautiful—a placid sheet of water sheltered in the woodlands with a shingly shore is not what you expected to find just off the road.

Return along the way you came on the main road back to the A.A. box, then follow the right-hand fork until you come to the turning on the right for Boat of Garten. A few yards this side of the turning you see what appears to be a farm road on the left; follow it, and it leads you through the wilderness of the old Deisher timber operations. After you have crossed the crest of the hill you see across the valley to the hills that guard the Dava Moor. This forest road brings you down to the metalled road where you turn to the left to come to Carrbridge. Just before entering the village you pass the scene of timber operations carried out by lumberwomen during the war.

Eighth day.

THE SLOCHD

Route in brief : Walk *via* Beananach and Sluggan—Dalnahaitnach to Slochd road—Slochd summit-road or hill-side to Carrbridge.

Walking distance : 13 miles.

Map : Ordnance Survey 1″ scale, No. 38.

At one time Carrbridge stood in the midst of woodlands, but now much of the timber has been cut down with the result that the little community of houses on the main road to Inverness is swept by the four winds. It is, however, a splendid walking centre, and a place where you could spend an excellent holiday. The Carrbridge Hotel offers the best of Highland hospitality.

The River Dulnan passes through the village on its way from the hills to join the Spey, and, after a period of heavy rain in the season, anybody with almost any kind of line may lift out salmon from the pool at the bridge which carries the main road.

From this bridge, follow the station road, but, instead of turning up to the station, keep straight on past where the Canadian lumbermen's camp was during the war. Then past Beananach (the area headquarters of the Newfoundland lumbermen during the war) and on for quite a few miles to the road-end, or what seems to be the road-end. In winter the snow lies deep in these parts, and the winds sweep down unmercifully from the heights. This road-end is called Dalnahaitnach, and, just beyond, you see a wooden bridge which puts you in the direction of the main road to Inverness. You reach the road at the cutting known as the Slochd Muic. Turn to the left, towards Inverness, as far as the summit, and then return to Carrbridge along the main road, or by following the moorlands on your left. About a mile north of Carrbridge you come to the crest of the hill, and spread out before you is the majesty of the Cairngorms. In the centre of this mighty panorama of mountains you see the huge V-shaped cleft that marks the Lairig Ghru Pass. Here, in this range, are gathered all but one of Scotland's mountains over 4,000 feet. Some time ago a writer mentioned that Lochnagar was higher than Ben Nevis; actually the height of Lochnagar does not allow the inclusion of the mountain in the select band of those of over 4,000 feet.

Ninth day.

DAVA MOOR

Route in brief: Carrbridge—Duthil—Craig an Righ—Lochindorb—Dava Station—Glascoile—Grantown.

Walking distance: 15 miles to Dava Station; 23 miles to Grantown.

Map: Ordnance Survey 1″ scale, No. 38.

At the cross-roads in Carrbridge, one road leads to Grantown-on-Spey. Go this way for about two miles until you come to the turning, on the left, at Duthil. This is the moorland route over Dava, where you cross the felled woodlands of Duthil, and then approach the escarpment of Craig an Righ on your right. The screes of this hill sweep down to two moorland lochans skirted by the road. After this you top the rise, where a wide vista of rolling uplands, stretching beyond the loch, carries the eye to the horizon. In the middle distance you see the lonely Lochindorb. On a small island in the loch is the remains of an extensive castle which figures as a royal castle in the history of Scotland. The rough, unfenced moorland road pushes across the bogs and, after a while, you come to the turning, on the right, which brings you to Lochindorb. At the beginning of the loch you see a by-way, on your right at Drumray; it leads to a path that goes across a section of the Dava Moor *via* a small pool marked on the map as Loch an't Sithean and to the Foal's Well. From there the path brings you to Garton Maggie, and so to Grantown. This is the alternative to continuing by the road which curves and zigzags across the moor to the main road at Dava Station.

If you have had enough of walking you can return by train from Dava to Grantown. Failing that, you have a total of twenty-three miles of walking to Grantown.

Perhaps the best of all suggestions is to lunch by the shores of Lochindorb and then go by way of Dava Moor track from Drumray over to the Foal's Well.

As you reach the approaches of Grantown you pass the policies of Castle Grant where rhododendrons make a colour picture in season.

Tenth day.

REST DAY

There are a number of easy excursions in the vicinity, but do not undertake anything strenuous as you have yet to face the Lairig Ghru expedition. Perhaps the best suggestion for to-day is to picnic in the little valley where Huntly's Cave is situated. Follow the Forres road for about three miles (this is along the road you walked yesterday), then turn to the right down to the valley where, for part of the way, the route is lined with raspberry bushes.

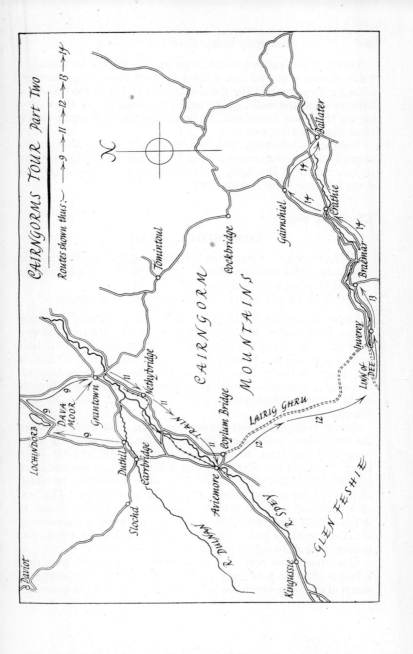

Down in the valley you come to what is known as Huntly's Cave, where it is said the second Earl of Huntly hid himself after fighting against the Covenanters. If you want to add a little more to the walk, continue, by the road out of the valley across the open moorland, to Ballinlagg and the main valley road back to Grantown.

Another interesting, but comparatively short, walk is to climb to the Jubilee cairn on the Cromdale Hills. Go by bus to Cromdale in the Spey valley and begin the climb of the open hill-side from the bus stop.

Eleventh day.

TOMINTOUL ROAD

Route in brief : Grantown—Tomintoul Road—Toperfettle —Revack—Old Military Road—Corriechullie—Nethybridge. *Walking distance :* 9 miles. *Map :* Ordnance Survey 1″ special map, " Cairngorms."

Leave Grantown by the Cromdale road, crossing the Spey by the Two Shires' Bridge. After passing Grantown railway station, you come to the right-hand turning uphill that points the way to Tomintoul. This route is yet another of the many military roads in the Highlands. Ascending all the while, you pass Toperfettle Farm, with Revack Woods on the right, felled during the war, but still called Revack Woods.

About four miles out from Grantown, and after crossing the watershed, you have a very extensive view, across a comparatively flat land, to the Cairngorms where, not far from Loch Avon, is the Shelter Stone where free accommodation is available all the year round. The accommodation provided consists of the shelter afforded by a group of rocks. The first of a series of visitors' books was left at the Shelter Stone in August 1924 and this book is now a treasured possession of the Cairngorm Club. The first signature in the book was that of Ishbel, daughter of Ramsay Macdonald.

One quotation reads: " Last night a party of two men arrived after we had gone to bed. The stone thus sheltered seven of us. Five lay in the large room and two in the entrance-hall. It is well in a party of this size to bring along one or two whose faces won't spoil by being jammed and scraped against the walls of the shelter."

Follow the road across the tableland and, in time, you come to Nethybridge. *En route* there is a left-hand turning that leads to Dorback Lodge on the Braes of Abernethy. From here, one path goes to the Bridge of Brown on the Tomintoul road, another through the hills to Glen Avon. Here you have a track north to Tomintoul and south to Cock Bridge. At Nethybridge, go by train to Aviemore to be ready, the next day, for the journey through the Lairig Ghru. Accommodation is available at the Dell, Inverdruie (*en route* Aviemore–Coylum Bridge), if you write in advance.

When you start the Lairig Ghru walk, inform the folk at the house where you stayed overnight of the actual route you intend to follow.

Twelfth day.

THE LAIRIG GHRU

Route in brief : Aviemore—Inverdruie—Coylum Bridge—Cairngorms Club Foot-bridge—Summit of Pass (2,733 feet)—Glen Dee—Pools of Dee—Devil's Point—Linn of Dee—Inverey.

Walking distance : 23 miles.

Map : Ordnance Survey 1″ special map, " Cairngorms."

When working out the details of this tour beforehand, not only should you study your maps carefully, but you should read the Scottish Mountaineering Club's *Guide to the Cairngorms*. To mountain lovers, this and other mountain guides are treasured possessions.

In addition to carrying a map you should, most certainly, carry a compass. Perhaps the best time of the year for attempting the Lairig Ghru is from May to July. Later than July you come to the stalking season, 20th August onwards. After that date do not make any ascents without previous enquiry. A tent is, of course, a useful addition to your kit if you intend staying in the hills overnight.

This strenuous excursion starts from Aviemore station.

Almost opposite the Youth Hostel the road branches from the main highway, following under the railway line and over the river.   Then, a mile or two of the road, and you are at Coylum Bridge with the bonny cottage beside it.   The road to the left is a quiet by-way which meanders past a green-fringed loch to Boat of Garten and Nethybridge.   At another time this road is worth exploring, but to-day you are heading for the Lairig Ghru.   At Coylum Bridge a signpost points the way to the right and, at once, you are set on the way to the summit.   Follow the track near the burn and, after about two miles, you come to the Cairngorms' Club bridge.   You cross the stream here.   At first a broad footway shows you the path and, after about a mile, another signpost indicates that the track is to the right.   From here to the top is just a steady ascent—five miles of it—and then you have reached the summit of the pass (2,733 feet).   Pray for a good day. You will need it, and if the visibility is satisfactory you will have a view never to be forgotten.   Many people have followed this route before and described their experiences.   I leave you to make your own experiences.

From the summit you descend to Glen Dee and then, below the Pools of Dee, cross to the left of the burn.   After a while, and about opposite the Devil's Point, the track divides, both arms taking you to your destination, but it is claimed that the path to the left is the better and more interesting route.   By following the left-hand way you come to Glen Luibeg and Derry Lodge and so to the Linn of Dee. This is your first real link with civilisation, and one more mile of walking and you are at Inverey, your destination for the night.

Thirteenth day.

INVEREY TO BRAEMAR

Five miles only of walking to-day and that will be quite enough.   Not only that, but remember that you have another day of walking to-morrow to end the tour.

The short route from Inverey to Braemar has been referred to, in reverse, at the beginning of this tour.   So it will suffice to say that to-day you walk to Braemar and stay overnight.

Fourteenth day.

THE GAIRNSHIEL

Route in brief : Various routes along the Dee valley and on to Aberdeen.

Walking distance : About 10 miles.

Map : Ordnance Survey 1″ scale, No. 38.

This is the last day of the tour and it is desirable to finish the day at Ballater or, if you are returning south of the Border, it is better to stay overnight in Aberdeen.

You have three possibilities before you to-day.

1. Walk from Braemar along the Ballater road as far as the entrance to Invercauld House. A few yards past the gates you turn left, and, after about a quarter of a mile, you follow the by-way on the right to Inver whence you can continue by bus to Ballater—6 miles walking.

2. Go by bus to Crathie. Visit the church and Balmoral, and then walk to Ballater along the South Deeside road— 7 miles' walking.

3. Go by bus to Crathie and walk *via* the north road. This is a rough and wild road without much traffic. This road leads you to the Gairnshiel where one road goes over the Glas-choile to Cock Bridge but you continue eastwards along the switchback road to Glen Gairn, where you go to the North Deeside road at Bridge of Gairn. At the main road turn to the left, when about half a mile of walking will bring you to Ballater.

The third suggestion is the one recommended. You could send your rucksack on in advance by bus to Ballater and so save carrying it. This old road from Crathie rises to the open moorlands and well above the timber-line and gives you some of the best views of the Cairngorms.

A " COMMANDO " TOUR

This is a special Cairngorms' excursion to be undertaken as a strenuous three-day alternative to the routes given on days ten to twelve inclusive.

No responsibility can be accepted for giving the outline of this tour, but it is emphasised that these three days are really tough going and should be undertaken only by the hardiest and most experienced trampers. Do not for a minute think the conditions are being exaggerated. If you do not believe that they are very severe, read the following quotation from " Tramp Royal's " experience : " I reached the summit of the Lairig Ghru; reached it to be hurled bodily back by a door of wind slamming in my face. Again I tried; again and yet again. But the pass was impassable. It was bricked up by an invisible brick wall of too galloping velocity."

That should be enough to convince you that it is tough going. Carry a good rucksack and a light-weight tent, a compass, plenty of food and do not go alone.

Here is the route given in the barest outline as an alternative to days ten to twelve.

Tenth day.

Walk, from Aviemore, up the long road to Coylum Bridge, and then continue up the lesser road ahead which leads to the V-shaped cleft in the mountains. Cross the Cairngorms' Club foot-bridge, and continue along a broad path which deteriorates to a narrow track through the heather to the pass. At the summit follow the March Burn, to the left, to Lochan Buidhe, and continue by the stream flowing out of the lochan to the Shelter Stone at the south end of Loch Avon. Here you stay the night.

Eleventh day.

Walk round the north side of Loch Avon for about a mile or so. Then ascend to the summit of Cairngorm (4,084 feet). Follow to the south-west *via* Cairn Lochan (3,983 feet) and Lochan Buidhe. Then, south by the ridge, to Ben Macdhui (4,296 feet). Descend north-east to the Shelter Stone for your second night.

Twelfth day.

Walk to the Lairig Ghru and the Pools of Dee, and climb in a south-westerly direction to the summit of Braeriach (4,248 feet). Follow the ridge in a southerly horse-shoe fashion, by

Einach Cairn and Wells of Dee, to Cairn Toul (4,241 feet). Descend to the Pools of Dee and down to the Linn of Dee and so to Inverey where you will stay overnight.

Thirteenth day.

After the strenuous days on the hills make this an easy day and be content with the short walk to Braemar.

XII

THE GREY MOUNTAINS

INTRODUCTION

THIS is the district of the Monadhliath Mountains—the Grey Mountains. You start the tour high up in the Highlands in a bleak wilderness of mountains and lochs, and the first day finds you following the old road that General Wade's men, under Leggatt, cut through and over the hills, over the Corrieyairack Pass. This is not such a famous pass to the tramper as the Lairig Ghru, but Inglis Ker claims that from the summit you have the finest view in Scotland. Many vantage points claim this distinction but in this case it seems justified.

From Fort Augustus to Inverness you follow a maze of little-known by-ways where you might imagine the road-makers used a corkscrew to plan the roads. There are many lochs in this district, lochs whose names seldom if ever appear in the guide-books. After Inverness, you cross the hills to the Findhorn and then, as far as possible, follow the course of the river through the hills to the plain which reaches to the sea.

Finally you have more highlands and woodlands to cross and this time with the Cairngorms as a background.

These tramping grounds are away from the more popular and well-known routes and introduce you to places of which you have probably never heard.

Read *The New Road*, by Neil Munro. It deals with the building of the Corrieyairack Military Road. Also read *The Flight of the Heron*, by D. K. Broster.

First day.

Travel to Newtonmore on the main Inverness line.

Second day.

THE CORRIEYAIRACK PASS

Route in brief : Newtonmore—Laggan—Blargie—Shirrabeg
—Glen Shirra Lodge—St. George's Bridge—Mealgarbha—
Corrieyairack—Summit of the Pass (2,507 feet)—Culachy
Forest—River Tarff—Fort Augustus.

Walking distance : 24 miles. Traverse of pass—4 hours.

Map : Ordnance Survey 1″ scale, No. 42.

This route is the remains of the military road built by Leggatt
under General Wade a few years before the '45 rebellion and
used by Prince Charlie and his men with good effect. As
General Cope and his men marched to Inverness from Dalwhinnie, the Young Pretender and his men marched through
the Corrieyairack to Dalwhinnie on their way south.

The road has long since ceased to be used for wheeled
traffic, but the track is still well defined and is not difficult to
follow.

Travel by bus from Newtonmore to Laggan on the Fort
William road. After alighting from the bus do not cross the
Spey Bridge, but, instead, follow the by-way and continue up-
hill, and more or less in line with the stream. This by-way
leads to the River Spey and follows alongside it for a
while. Then you cross the river to come to Shirrabeg and
Glen Shirra Lodge. You are now all set for the Corrieyairack
Pass.

Keep to the river-side as far as the cottage called Mealgarbha ;
beyond this the track leads to the summit of the pass and then
descends to the ford at the River Tarff. After this crossing
you traverse a barren moorland, and then, after the woodlands
of Culachy Forest, you reach the main road where a walk of
less than two miles brings you to Fort Augustus. There is a
monastery at Fort Augustus, and it is no uncommon sight
to see one or more of the monks on the nearby roads. The
Caledonian Canal is carried through the village by a series
of locks from Loch Ness to the higher levels of the valley
leading towards Fort William.

The walk through the Pass is long and arduous, and,
although not as stiff as the Lairig Ghru walk, it will, nevertheless, test your stamina, especially as it is your first day of

walking. It is an excursion only for the summer season. The climatic conditions can be unbelievably severe. Anyone who has had to live and work in these wild places knows, only too well, how very hard a winter's day can be.

Third day.

WHITEBRIDGE

Route in brief: Fort Augustus—Wade's Military Road— Glen Doe—Loch Tarff—Strath Errick—Whitebridge.

Walking distance: 10 miles.

Map: Ordnance Survey 1″ scale, No. 42.

The long trek of yesterday calls for easier going to-day. Ten miles will be your tally and so there is no real need to leave until after midday. To start with, you have a long climb out of Fort Augustus along the road that sweeps up- wards towards Whitebridge. As you ascend you have a wider and yet wider view of Loch Ness, but, perhaps, the most impressive is from the foot of the road where you have an uninterrupted view to the grey horizon where hills, loch and sky merge. It is a scene that inspires visitors to exclaim that no other place in the world can compare with it. It is, indeed, superb.

At the head of the road you have a final glimpse of the loch, which is so deep that it never freezes, and then the route dips down to Glen Doe where a crumbling bridge stands as a reminder of the old road and its attendant risks.

You start climbing again and see, on your right, the long waterfall of Glen Doe. The road, recently re-made, follows the line of General Wade's road and takes you all the way to Whitebridge. At the top of the rise, where the road narrows and there are crossing places for traffic, you come to Loch Tarff. Even on a sunny day the place has a grey look and is a fitting scene for the Grey Mountains range. After skirting the loch, where the road surface is only a few inches above the water level, you turn sharply uphill and make the long ascent across the face of the moorland with the long glen on your right. This glen acts as a catch-basin for a small loch called Loch nan Eun. Eventually you reach the highest point in to-day's walk and, both in front and behind, you have a

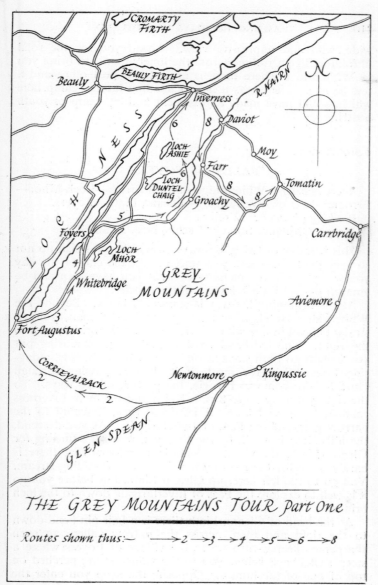

THE GREY MOUNTAINS TOUR Part One

Routes shown thus:— ⟶2 ⟶3 ⟶4 ⟶5 ⟶6 ⟶8

wide, wild and impressive view. Ahead you see the road unfolding, like a ribbon across the lonely moor, to bring you to Whitebridge where there is an hotel, a post office and a few houses. There was a large Canadian lumber camp here which would have made an excellent holiday camp or youth hostel.

Fourth day.

FALLS OF FOYERS

Route in brief : Whitebridge—Strath Errick—Loch Mhòr—Errogie—Pass of Inverfarigaig—Gleann Liath—Foyers.
Walking distance : 12 miles.
Maps : Ordnance Survey 1" scale, Nos. 37 and 42.

This is a day of twisty by-ways on which you finish up not so very far from where you started. At the end of the day you will glory in the memory of what you have seen and be amazed that so little is known of the district.

At the beginning the way is somewhat bleak. Beyond the Whitebridge Hotel, after a steep dip in the road, you go straight ahead in line with the river and, at the bridge, turn to the right. The left-hand road is well worth exploring but you cannot go both ways at once, so to the right it is, alongside Loch Mhòr for most of its length, passing through Gorthleck to come to Errogie, the parting of the ways. To the right you may go to Strath Nairn and the main Inverness road, but you will take the left-hand turn, downhill to the narrow gorge of the Pass of Inverfarigaig. As you descend, the hills close in until, by the time you reach the turning for Gleann Liath, the wooded defile is so narrow that there is barely space for the road by the side of the tumbling stream. You go to the left here, up Gleann Liath, but before you go it is well to explore the Pass of Inverfarigaig down to the loch bridge.

At the head of Gleann Liath there is a hair-pin bend down to the right and then, across the narrow valley, an even sharper corkscrew-turn up to the village of Foyers where a steep switchback brings you to the village store, perched on top of one of the humps. Opposite the shop you enter the woodlands and there, paths lead to the edge of the precipice which drops down to the gorge where the waters of Foyers tumble to the loch. It is well worth while to descend by the road down to the loch-side and go through the farm to the vantage point where you see the gorge from below.

Fifth day.

WALKING THROUGH THE HILLS

Route in brief : Boleskine—Inverfarigaig—Dun Deardail—Bochruben—Loch Cé Glais—Loch Dun Seilcheig—Loch Ruthven—Strath Nairn—East Croachy.

Walking distance : 13 miles.

Map : Ordnance Survey 1″ scale, No. 37.

The route to Inverfarigaig, in line with the glen, is high above the loch when you leave Foyers but, by the time you reach the entrance to the pass, you are very near the water level. The stretch of road before you to reach Inverfarigaig might well be named " The primrose way," because, in season, the road verges fringing the woodlands are carpeted with primroses. Do not turn up the Pass of Inverfarigaig, but cross the bridge and follow the road up the incline and round the bend where you see a by-way on the right; it takes you into the mouth of the pass and then climbs up and out between the rocks to the moorland and a little-used route to Loch Cé Glais. It seems a deserted and desolate region, yet there is a school-house situated not far from the loch. Here is a district that is almost completely isolated in winter, and even in summer time it is quite an occasion to see a vehicle on the loch-side road. The loch itself is only a small sheet of water and, as soon as you have topped the short rise, you look down on the much larger expanse of Loch Dun Seilcheig. It is not long since you left Loch Ness and the deep fault of the Great Glen, and it seems strange that such a large stretch of water should be found on this plateau above the glen.

Immediately before reaching the loch, where the road curves downhill to the left, you see a track on your right barred by a gate. This is your way. You descend almost to the loch and then comes another wandering way *via* Loch Ruthven to Strath Nairn at East Croachy. Hereabouts is a fisherman's howff—Flicherty Hotel—by the side of a lochan.

Sixth day.

DRUMASHIE MOOR

Route in brief : East Croachy—Brinmore—Loch a' Chlach-ain—Loch Dun Seilcheig—Loch Ashie—Drumashie Moor—Scaniport—Inverness.

Walking distance : 13 miles to Scaniport; 17 miles to Inverness.

Map : Ordnance Survey 1″ scale, No. 37.

Proceed from East Croachy along the Strath Nairn road in the direction of Farr and, when under the shadow of the Brin Rock, turn left for the way across the moors to Inverness. Looking back you see the " Shrinking Mountain." When walking in the opposite direction you see a knobbly hill called Stac Gorm, but as you approach the hill it seems to decrease in size until it appears to merge with the rocky mass of the general hill-side.

The road you follow to the left divides after about two miles, and here you go to the left again and skirt the pool of Loch a' Chlachain before coming to the shore of Loch Dun Seilcheig, which you saw yesterday from the other end. Soon after leaving this loch you come to another but nothing like so big—Loch Ashie; so to the cross-roads on Drumashie Moor. Go ahead and, very soon, down the zigzag way, you come in sight of Loch Ness with the mountains rising almost sheer from the water's edge to 1,600 feet. You are now looking down at the head of the loch and will say good-bye to this part of the country. Earlier in the week you looked up the long vista of the glen from Fort Augustus and then you came again to the shores of the loch at Foyers. Now you see the loch for the last time and, after descending to the main Inverness road at Scaniport, you continue the remaining four miles to Inverness either by foot or bus.

The last three days have introduced you to a district little known to most people, an area that calls for a book all to itself. Some day perhaps it will receive the attention it deserves.

Seventh day.

REST DAY

Inverness has plenty to offer for a rest day. You have done five days' continuous walking and so it is time you gave your feet a rest. You can go in search of the Inverness accent and pay a visit to the cattle market. Guide-books usually content themselves with the historical background of a place, and a cattle market seldom seems to be worthy of attention. Yet here, at the cattle market of Inverness, you will meet the farmers from the shire and will learn what the Inverness-shire accent sounds like. The farmer and his family in this district are friendly folk. Always when one ends a visit the parting words will be " haste ye back."

A cemetery on a hill called Tomnahurich is referred to as a place of interest for tourists, but the small hill on which the Castle stands is the finest place in Inverness. The Castle itself is not of any great age and does not fit into the picture with complete harmony. You have travelled far and walked through some of the wildest scenes the country had to offer, and you will feel in coming to Inverness that it should represent the spirit of Scotland. You have such a feeling when standing at this vantage point.

From the Castle, descend to the river-side and explore the Ness gardens. Then turn about and walk on the north side of the river, on the estuary-side, as far as the Kessock Ferry. Whether or not you cross the ferry does not matter, because you have a worth-while view of the Northland here.

There is not space enough to give a detailed story of Inverness, but you are recommended to visit the museum in Castle Wynd. Number 43 Castle Street is the site of the house where the Dowager Lady Macintosh was hostess, in turn, to Prince Charlie and the Duke of Cumberland. Church Street also contains, hidden in a narrow close, the oldest house in Inverness.

H. V. Morton, in his *In Search of Scotland*, has stories to tell of Inverness, but what must the folk of that city think of him for describing bagpipes as " bags of woe " ?

Eighth day.

OVER THE HILLS TO THE FINDHORN

Route in brief: Inverness—Bus to Farr—Strath Nairn—
Loch Farr—Glen Kyllachy—River Findhorn.

Walking distance: 13 miles.

Maps: Ordnance Survey 1″ scale, Nos. 37 and 38.

Old roads were made for trampers but, to-day, you are
offered a route that would come up to anyone's standard.
Travel by service bus to Farr in Strath Nairn, where you leave
the main road almost at once and turn to your left (with your
back to Inverness) to come to Loch Farr. Beyond the loch
the road rises to the rolling uplands, bare and quiet. You
cross over the watershed and descend Glen Kyllachy to Strath
Nairn and the River Findhorn, which you follow for the next
few days. You reach the river-side in the glen between
Coignafearn and the Tomatin Bridge, which carries the road
over the river. This erection has been referred to as " one
of the Road Board's embodiments of modernism " which is
really a polite way of saying that it is very ugly.

The River Findhorn is worthy of much more attention than
can be given here. Fortunately, Thomas Henderson, in his
book, *The Findhorn*, tells you all that you want to know.
His book will help you considerably in planning your holiday.

High up in the tangle of hills above Coignafearn the River
Findhorn starts its career, where two hill streams, called Eskin
and Abhainn Cro Clach, meet. If you trace the route on the
Ordnance Map you will see that there is a possible route from
Whitebridge up the glen and over the head-waters of the Eskin.
It was somewhere up here, surely, that D. K. Broster laid
one of her scenes in *The Flight of the Heron.*

Go down Strath Nairn, by the side of the stream, to Tomatin
Bridge and turn to the left, along the main highway through
Strath Dearn to Tomatin. Seek accommodation at local
cottages, or possibly at Freeburn Hotel, farther on towards
Inverness. There is a bus service from Tomatin to Inverness,
so if you are unable to obtain accommodation in Tomatin
go to Inverness for the night and return to Tomatin the next
morning.

Ninth day.

THE SLOCHD

Route in brief : Tomatin—Findhorn Bridge—Slochd Road —Summit of the Slochd (1,327 feet)—General Wade's Road —Dalnahown—Findhorn viaduct—Soilshan—Soilshan Wood —Findhorn Bridge—Tomatin.
Walking distance : 7 miles.
Map : Ordnance Survey 1″ scale, No. 38.

Here is an easy day to fit in between two more strenuous days. You can, however, extend your walking by exploring on the hills above the Slochd where herds of wild goats roam. The animals usually keep well back from the road, but in winter, when you occasionally see them, they look anything but timid, especially the male ones with their long curved horns.

From Tomatin village follow the main road in the direction of Carrbridge and, after a little more than two miles, you reach the summit of the Slochd. At the notice-board marking the summit, traverse the hill-side to the north to come to the old military road. Cross the first track you come to and continue a little higher up, not too high, however, because the highest point on the military road is not much more than 1,000 feet. And now you go, in a northerly direction, back to Tomatin across the open hill-side, descending gradually to the Findhorn at Dalnahown. Turn to the left at Dalnahown and follow the track under the high railway viaduct, and through the Soilshan Woods, to the main road again. These woodlands make a suitable place for a picnic.

Back again on the main road, you turn in the direction of Inverness and soon are back again at Tomatin.

If you want to do a more extended walk to-day, follow the road from Tomatin Bridge up to Coignafearn and the head-waters of the Findhorn. Here is a maze of hills in which to wander and you can use up as many miles as you feel inclined. It seems that the river is notorious for its sudden rises and falls. A heavy downpour in the region of the head-waters may start a spate of peaty waters roaring through the narrows of the Streens.

Tenth day.

THROUGH THE STREENS

Route in brief : Dalmagarry—Milton of Moy—River Findhorn—Bucket Bridge—Dulsie Bridge—Ferness.

Walking distance : 17 miles to Dulsie Bridge; 22 miles to Ferness.

Map : Ordnance Survey 1″ scale, No. 38.

John Buchan declared that the finest section of the Findhorn was through the Streens from Dalmagarry to Dulsie Bridge, and so there should be no fault to find with this as the choice for to-day. It is a long day, but there is no alternative. Once you leave Dalmagarry you must go right on to Dulsie Bridge, there are no half measures.

Continue along the main road in the direction of Inverness, passing Freeburn Hotel where, at one time, a big cattle fair was held, and so on past Tomatin Distillery.

Beyond Freeburn, you top the rise in the road, where the snow lies deep in winter, and descend to the bridge at Dalmagarry. Here you bear away to the right, along the track that takes you back to the side of the Findhorn. Before branching off the main road you may wish to go on another short mile to see Loch Moy. It is worth the little extra walking. There are two islands in the loch. The very small one—Eilan nan Clach—nearer the road, was formerly used as a prison; the larger—Isle of Moy—contains the crumbling ruins of a castle and there is a monument, erected in 1824, in memory of the Macintosh family.

The track from Dalmagarry brings you to the river at Milton of Moy and goes on to Ruthven. From now on the valley narrows and the river is hemmed in a narrow defile. It is advisable to cross the river at Shenachie by the Bucket or Cradle Bridge (if it is still there). There is a path on the left side of the river through the Streens, but it is very narrow and dangerous. Follow the right bank through the Streens.

A short distance after Shenachie you cross the boundary that divides Inverness and Nairn, and continue, following the stream through the hills. The route is there to follow all the way to Dulsie Bridge. Check as you go with the

W. A. Poucher, F.R.P.S.

THE LAIRIG GHRU

THE PASS OF INVERFARIGAIG

THE STREENS, RIVER FINDHORN

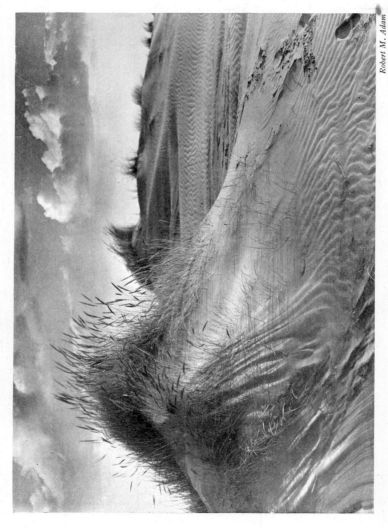

CULBIN SANDS

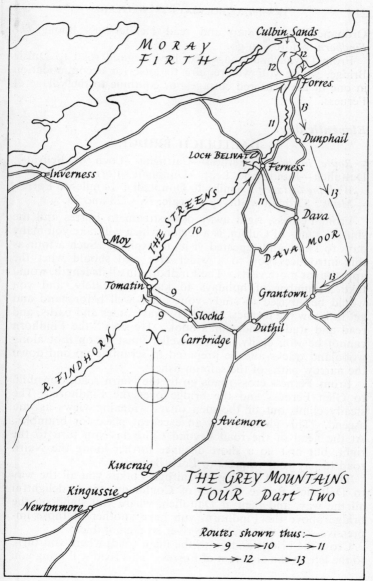

MORAY
FIRTH

Culbin Sands

12

12 *12*

Forres

13

11

Dunphail

LOCH BELIVAT

Ferness

Inverness

13

11

THE STREENS

10

Dava

DAVA MOOR

Moy

13

Tomatin

9

Grantown

9

Slochd

Duthil

Carrbridge

R. FINDHORN

N

Aviemore

Kincraig

THE GREY MOUNTAINS
TOUR Part Two

Kingussie

Newtonmore

Routes shown thus:—
⟶ *9*   ⟶ *10*   ⟶ *11*
⟶ *12*   ⟶ *13*

Ordnance Survey map and read Henderson's book, *The Findhorn*, before you go.

From Drynachan Lodge you have a good road to Dulsie Bridge, where you will require to look for accommodation in one of the scattered cottages, or continue to the village of Ferness.

Eleventh day.

DALTULICH BRIDGE

Route in brief : Ferness—Cairnglas—Loch of Belivat—Daltulich—Randolph's Leap—Dunphail—Forres.

Walking distance : 6 miles to Dunphail ; 14 miles to Forres.

Maps : Ordnance Survey 1″ scale, Nos. 28 and 38.

From Ferness, right away downstream to Forres and the shifting sands of Culbin, is a region which will take you many days to know and repeated visits to explore. Such a tour as this introduces you to a wider area and should whet the appetite for more visits. The Findhorn, in all its length, would take a number of holidays to know intimately, and you would be advised to study your maps well beforehand and get to know the district. Study by-way routes and paths, and read and study Henderson's book. He says " the Findhorn cannot be won easily. The traveller must go on foot along woodland tracks and be prepared to scramble up and down the narrow paths of the salmon fishers."

From Ferness cross-roads go by the Nairn road, downhill, to Glen Ferness and the bridge over the Findhorn. The steady climb out of the glen offers widening views as you ascend. This glen, too, is an excellent place for brambles. At the head of the road beyond Cairnglas you turn to the right, but first go a short distance farther along the Nairn road to pay your respects to Loch Belivat.

The right-hand turning at Cairnglas takes you all the way to Daltulich Bridge by way of Coulmany. It is delightful all the way, and then at Daltulich, where you stand on the bridge above the Findhorn, you have another of those impressive scenes that make the river so memorable.

Cross the bridge and go to the main road, where you turn, to the left, in the direction of Forres. This road will bring you to the road-junction, but first you traverse the woodlands and visit Randolph's Leap. The route twists downhill, and then winds uphill to the road junction at Dunphail. You have now come to the plains stretching to the sea and about eight miles of walking brings you to the town of Forres.

Twelfth day.

THE CULBIN SANDS

Measured in miles you will not go very far to-day, but as you have followed the line of the Findhorn almost from its source you should end up by going to the mouth of the river at Findhorn Bay and, in particular, see the Culbin Sands. Although the miles will not be many the going will be very hard because there is nothing so wearisome as ploughing through the fine sands of the dunes of Culbin. Be assured, however, that the visit is well worth while.

From Forres, cross the suspension bridge and go, *via* Dalvey, to Kintessock and on to the dunes. The Forestry Commission is planting here with the object of binding and holding the sands. It is very slow work, however, and much of the labour is undone by the continuous shifting of the sands. This district, now covered by an ocean of sand, was once a fertile part of Morayland but, more than two hundred years ago, a terrible twenty-four hours of drift buried the manor of Kinnaird of Culbin and all the neighbouring houses. Since that day nothing has existed except an ever-moving waste of finely powdered sand which is sensitive to the least whisper of wind. When the wind blows strongly from the west the position of the pedestrian caught in the dunes can be dangerous. However, in spite of the toil of trudging through the sands, you will find it well worth while. Perhaps the best way to get the story of the sands is to speak to some local person who can tell you how the cultivated fields disappeared in the course of a day, and with what difficulty cattle were saved, so fast did the drifting sands gather.

From whence did the avalanche of sand come ? One supposition is that " the sand drift was caused by changes in the Firth, of which there are unmistakable proofs, and the sand was driven from various points along the shore eastwards from Nairn and Fort George when the old coastline was broken up."

Another sinister date in the history of the district is 1829, when the terrible August floods caused so much damage. In fact the event left such a deep impression that later events in local history are referred to as happening so many years " after the flood."

Not far from the Culbin Sands, and near to Brodie Station, is Hardmuir, the " blasted heath " where Macbeth and Banquo met the witches—" the three withered hags."

Thirteenth day.

DAVA MOOR

Route in brief : Route 1.—Forres—Dunphail Station—River Divie—Dava Moor Hill road—Ballinlagg—Grantown.
Walking distance : 15 miles.
Route 2.—Forres—Dava Station—Lochindorb—Duthil—Grantown.
Walking distance : 15 miles.
Maps : Ordnance Survey 1″ scale, Nos. 28 and 38.

From Dunphail railway station, follow the road south of the River Divie, a worthy tributary of the Findhorn. You now leave the main road and, going in the general direction of the river upstream, follow the old road that leads towards the head-waters of the Divie. Then follow the Ourack Burn where the track ends at a clump of trees (check with your map). You have about two miles of walking ahead, across the open moor, to reach the path again at Badahad. This track leads down to the Spey valley and, as you approach the valley, the track divides. The left-hand track takes you round by Ballinlagg to the Grantown road, while the right-hand fork goes down the glen and climbs up to the main road near Ballieward, about a mile and a half out from Grantown-on-Spey.

For route 2, you travel by train to Dava Station on the Grantown route. Outside the station you see the branch road which takes you across part of the Dava moor to Lochindorb and beyond, to join the north and south road crossing from Forres to Duthil. You turn left at the road-junction and face the six miles to the Carrbridge–Grantown road at Duthil. This route is described, in reverse, in the " Cairngorms Tour," ninth day.

At the road-junction of the Grantown road you travel by service bus to Grantown. There is a regular service from Carrbridge. This road-junction is near a desolate expanse of felled woodlands. Along the Duthil road the Newfoundlanders camped for at least three years during the war and extracted an extensive acreage of timber from the district. Much of the felled timber was used for pitwood, while part passed through the Carrbridge sawmill operated by the Canadian lumbermen.

The section of road between Duthil and Dulnanbridge, *en route* for Grantown, is very exposed, and in winter time is one of the first roads in the district to become impassable.

Fourteenth day.

GRANTOWN AND DISTRICT

This is the last day of the tour and you have the choice of various walks. You started the tour at Newtonmore and therefore you book a return ticket to Newtonmore and then return from Grantown to Newtonmore on a single ticket or travel by bus. There is a bus service from Grantown through to Newtonmore.

Of the various excursions the most appropriate for to-day is the one described in " The Cairngorms' Tour," eleventh day. This will give you a nine-mile walk, *via* the Tomintoul road and over the moors, and down to Nethybridge, whence you can return to Grantown by bus or continue to Aviemore. This latter place offers a variety of accommodation for an overnight stay, and the next morning you could join the main-line train for the journey south.

A second plan would be to travel by bus to Carrbridge, and undertake the walk given for the eighth day of " The Cairngorms Tour." This excursion takes you along the byway to Dalnahaitnach, and then across to the Slochd. Return to Carrbridge by way of the main road.

The Jubilee Cairn in the hills of Cromdale is another place to visit if you like, instead of the Slochd or the Nethybridge uplands.

The Corrieyairack is a very strenuous introduction to this tour, and if you feel it is too much to undertake, then start the tour at Fort Augustus and put in an extra day at Grantown and do one of the walks suggested. If you start at Fort Augustus you will travel by train to Inverness and then travel by bus along the shores of Loch Ness to Fort Augustus *via* Drumnadrochit. There is no passenger-train service to Fort Augustus.

Your first day might well be spent exploring the Fort Augustus end of the Corrieyairack Pass just as far as you feel able. One objection to this suggestion is that you must return by the same route and that is never very satisfactory. The better suggestion, therefore, if you start the tour at Fort Augustus, is to put in the day saved at Grantown-on-Spey.

INDEX